ADIRONDACK ROOTS

Stories of Hiking, History and Women

SANDRA WEBER

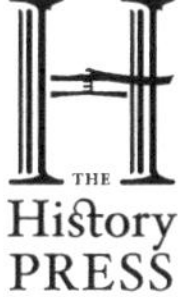

Published by The History Press
Charleston, SC 29403
www.historypress.net

Front cover and back cover, top: Sketches from the November 21, 1868 *Harper's Weekly. Drawn by Theodore T. Davis.*

Back cover, bottom: Summit of Mount Marcy. *Photo by Sandra Weber.*

First published 2011

Manufactured in the United States

ISBN 978.1.60949.364.6

Library of Congress Cataloging-in-Publication Data

Weber, Sandra, 1961-
Adirondack roots : stories of hiking, history, and women / Sandra Weber.
p. cm.
ISBN 978-1-60949-364-6
1. Adirondack Mountains (N.Y.)--History. 2. Adirondack Mountains (N.Y.)--Description and travel. I. Title.
F127.A2W36 2011
974.7'5--dc23
2011020367

Notice: The information in this book is true and complete to the best of our knowledge. It is offered without guarantee on the part of the author or The History Press. The author and The History Press disclaim all liability in connection with the use of this book.

To Dave

Contents

Contents

Acknowledgements

This book has been more than two decades in the making. It spans the entire lifetimes of my children. Through the years, my daughters grew, my adventures expanded and my writing progressed, taking me places I never imagined. Along the way, there were unexpected turns and crevasses and roots that tripped me, but that is life in the Adirondacks.

Life in the Adirondack community is also about helping one another. Many friends have aided my journey—hiking with me, swabbing my wounds, making me laugh and sharing research, stories and photos. I can't list all of your names, but I remember you and feel fortunate to count you as friends.

Thank you to the following publishers for originally publishing the writings presented in this book: *Adirondac*; *Adirondack Life*; *Adirondack Explorer*; Calkins Creek Books/Boyds Mills Press, Inc.; *New York State Conservationist*; Purple Mountain Press, Ltd.; *SCBWI Bulletin*; the *Sequel*; and *WOW (Wild Outdoor World)*. I am also grateful to those who supplied photos: Adirondack Collection, Saranac Lake Free Library; Adirondack Museum; Carl Heilman; L. John Van Norden; and the 1932 and 1980 Lake Placid Winter Olympic Museum.

Whitney Tarella championed this project from the beginning. Thank you to Whitney and the entire staff at The History Press for your support and your masterful skills in bringing this book to completion.

A special thank you to my daughters, Emily Anna and Marcy, for your patience and enduring love for the past twenty years. I know that my path was not always the easiest or soundest to follow, but I hope that this book helps you to understand.

Trail Tales

Hooked on History

The Adirondacks have so much to offer—magnificent mountains, long lakes and lush forests; rustic crafts, strong people and splendid history.

Yes, history. Not the history spouted in an eighth-grade social studies book. Nor the history told on television. I mean living, breathing, splinter-in-your-finger history. Like the kind you get exploring remnants of an old ski lodge at the top of Esther Mountain. Or the prickly lesson from interrogating a one-hundred-year-old spruce atop Mount Marcy. Or the messy work of inspecting a charred stump from the fire of 1903.

That's Adirondack history. Sometimes it's dirty business. Sometimes it's heart wrenching or humorous. Sometimes it's all wet, like the bit of history I plunged into at Avalanche Pass.

Last summer, I took a four-mile hike to one of the most spectacular spots in the Adirondacks. The sheer rock wall of Mount Colden drops into sparkling Avalanche Lake on one side, while the steep face of Avalanche Mountain slides down the other. Photographers love the view of Avalanche Lake. Rock climbers seek the cliffs and the Colden Trap Dike. Hikers appreciate the short passageway from Heart Lake to Lake Colden. Though the trail is rough in places, the route has been used by many people, including the legendary Matilda Fielding.

Guide Bill Nye led the rather "ample" Matilda, her husband and her niece up Mount Marcy and back through Avalanche Pass in 1868. To avoid getting wet, she rode on the shoulders of Mr. Nye. But like any proper lady,

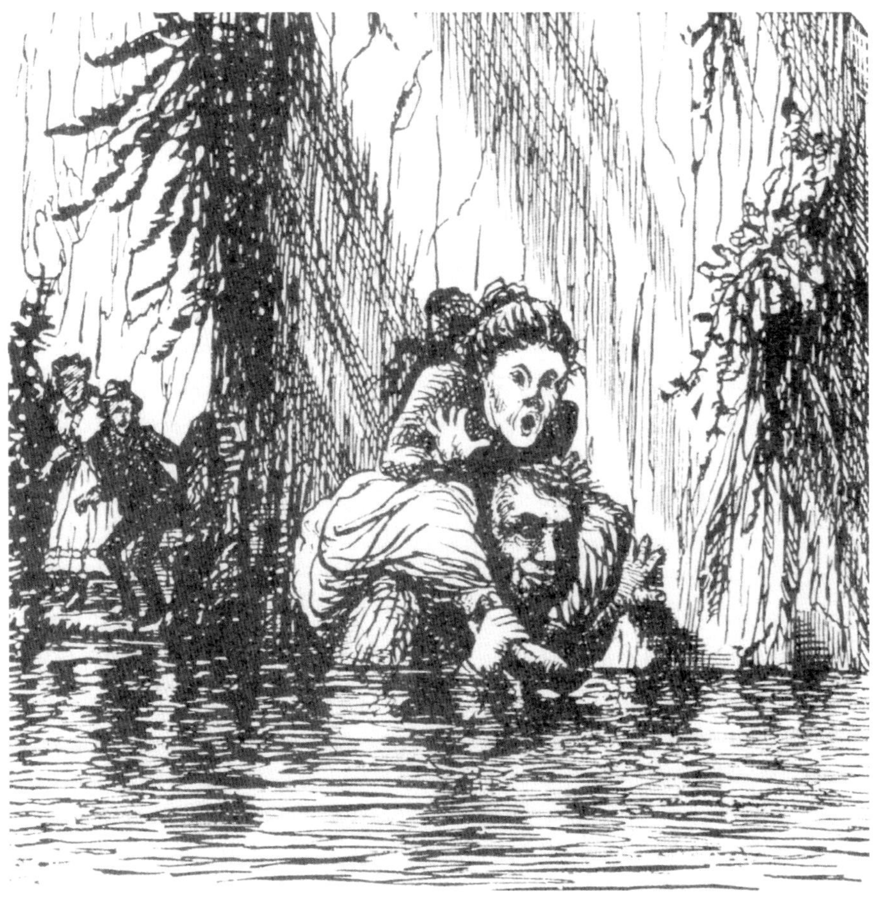

"Hitch-up Matilda!" *Sketch by Seneca Ray Stoddard.*

she did not clamp her legs tightly around his neck; instead, she slipped lower and lower down his back. Meanwhile, her husband stood on the shore laughing at the sight and yelling, "Hitch-up, Matilda! Hitch-up!"

Where exactly did this hilarious historic event take place? I scrambled over boulders, climbed up and down wooden ladders and squeezed through crevices in search of the spot now called "Hitch-up Matilda." Finally, I reached the place where the cliffs rise directly out of the water. A wooden boardwalk bolted to the cliff carries hikers across the water now. But it didn't carry me. I jumped into the lake and swam over to the walkway. Sure enough, there was a rock shelf hidden a few feet under the water. There was the shelf Bill Nye walked across while carrying Matilda.

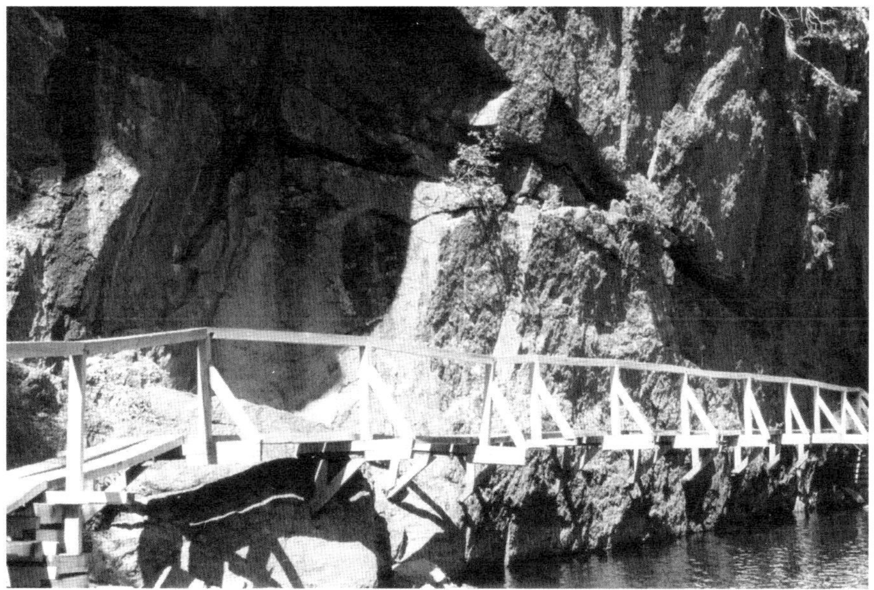

The present-day "Hitch-up Matilda" boardwalk in Avalanche Pass.

Now that I had found the shelf, I couldn't stop. I was curious about this Matilda lady. I went to the National Archives and looked at census records. I drove to Albany and examined old city directories. I looked at obituaries in the *New York Times*. And I found a woman named Matilda Fielding who lived in Brooklyn. She was married to a coach manufacturer who made business wagons of every description: circus, band chariots, baggage wagons and animal cages. Sure sounds wacky enough to be our Hitch-up Matilda!

Then one day, I discovered that Matilda's story wasn't as bizarre as it appeared. It seems that when the water was high along the carry trail between Upper and Lower Ausable Lakes, guide Monroe Holt used to carry the ladies on his back. It seems that Matilda wasn't so offbeat after all—other nineteenth-century ladies hitched-up as well. And so did men. Even Noah Porter, president of Yale College, wrapped his arms around the neck of Monroe Holt and climbed onto his back. "A funny sight it was," reported a witness to the scene. He looked very unlike "the Presiding Genius of Yale College."

Before I knew it, this hitching-up business whittled away a perfectly good month of summer. Of course, it's not the first time I've been hooked by Adirondack history. The legend of Esther McComb hooked me for two years. This fifteen-year-old farm girl supposedly attempted to climb

Whiteface Mountain in 1839 and accidently ascended a neighboring peak, which her mother later named Esther Mountain.

I tracked Esther for months. I searched libraries, museums, courthouses and cemeteries throughout upstate New York. In time, I found clues that convinced me that Esther existed, although her name was Combs, not McComb. And it seemed very likely that she climbed Esther Mountain, giving her the honor of being the first woman to ascend a high peak and the first—and only—woman to have a high peak named for her.

Then there were the three years I was caught up in the tragic love story of Jo Schofield and Henry Van Hoevenberg. And there's Mary Brown, wife of abolitionist John Brown. And forester Gifford Pinchot and hotelier Paul Smith. And so many others.

What is it that keeps tugging me into Adirondack history? I feel a connection to these stories and these people. It's not simply nostalgia. My connection is the land. The places where these people lived, worked and frolicked are still here. They are places that I can walk or swim to. They are places that hold relics of the past that I can see, touch and hear.

For me, Adirondack history isn't about memorizing dates and names and facts. It's about understanding and appreciating places and people. Not just people who are famous or rich or pretty, but people whose lives and work transformed a community or a landscape. Whether they discovered a mountain, quietly raised a family or simply hitched-up a guide's back, they contributed to the heritage of the Adirondack Mountains.

Lake Tear

Trekking to the Headwaters of the Hudson

Way up among the Adirondack peaks is a little pool asleep. Through the long winter it lies—a solid crystal almost—under the accumulating weight of many snows, barren of all life save that which, like itself, waits for the summer's sun to warm it into tardy being and bring with the rank green fringe its swarms of batrachian young.
—Seneca Ray Stoddard, 1885

Lake Tear of the Clouds remains as picturesque today as Seneca Ray Stoddard portrayed it more than one hundred years ago. Nestled between mountain peaks and circled by dark forests, the pool offers the perfect spot for a respite after a hard climb. Looking at the small pond, it's hard to believe that these are the headwaters of the mighty Hudson.

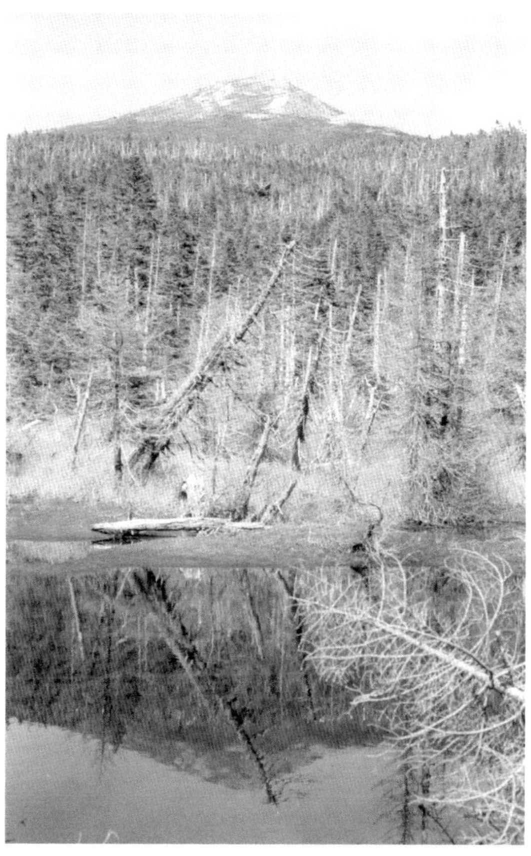

Mount Marcy overlooking Lake Tear of the Clouds.

Reaching Lake Tear's shore is no small feat, requiring a nine-mile walk through the Adirondack forest. I always wanted to visit it and so decided to make the trek this fine morning. Setting out from the deserted Upper Works, a principal trailhead that accesses the Adirondack High Peaks, I cross the twenty-foot-wide Calamity Brook and walk along an old logging road to Calamity Pond. A tall stone monument reminds me that entrepreneur David Henderson accidentally shot himself and died on this spot in 1845. I continue onward to a less ominous campsite.

After circling Flowed Lands, crossing the bridge at Lake Colden and wading across the Opalescent River, I pitch my tent. Throughout the night, I listen to a brook's soft babble, my excitement mounting at the prospect of reaching its source the next day: Lake Tear of the Clouds, headwaters of the Hudson River.

Morning clouds and dense fog beg me to wait for a day of summer sun, but I ignore them. I venture up the banks of the Opalescent, past the Flume. It is a tough pull, with a very crooked and snarled trail that requires me to climb over and under log after log.

Invisible droplets dampen my cheeks but not my mettle. I follow the ever-shrinking branch of the Hudson River along its wild course, ascending fifteen hundred feet in two hours. Here, the wide and mighty Hudson has transformed into a wee little creek—Feldspar Brook in name but as narrow as a rainspout and as shallow as a birdbath.

What it lacks in size, it makes up for in spirit. At this point, the water gushes into a stone basin that snares it for a moment before spilling it into a lower basin. The wild cascade continues on and on, rushing toward North Creek, Albany, Manhattan and eventually the Atlantic Ocean. Standing there, it dawns on me that this is the spontaneous birth of the Hudson.

I lift my head and look beyond the bustle into the eerie stillness. It's late morning, yet a gray mist gives the sense of sleepy dawn, as if the glaciers have just retreated. At last, I spy the little pool and the rank green fringe—the likely source of the vapors that ooze into my nostrils.

The eastern half of the pond is covered by puffy moss, pondweed and ashen tree skeletons. On the western shore, dark green spruce reflect their knurly forms onto the smooth open water. The bald gray heads of two rocks lurk in the middle. I can't help but notice that there are no air bubbles or flashes of fish fins. The pond, I'm told, has never been home to fish; some surmise that the stream is too steep to support much in the way of aquatic insect life and that spring meltwaters scour the streambeds.

Only two acres in size and less than three feet deep, the pond is essentially a bog. And like any bog, the open water will slowly be covered with a mat of moss and other plants. Lake Tear of the Clouds may one day become dry land, but that day is far away. For now, the water of Lake Tear rests at my feet, and Mount Marcy, the tallest mountain in the state, hovers one thousand feet above.

However, there is no view of Marcy today. The mountain is living up to its nickname, Cloudsplitter, with dripping clouds hanging just twenty feet above the calm surface of Lake Tear. In 1872, one of the lake's first known Caucasian visitors, state surveyor Verplanck Colvin, looked out at a similar scene and later wrote: "But how wild and desolate this spot!...First seen as we then saw it, dark and dripping with the moisture of the heavens, it seemed, on its minuteness and its prettiness, a veritable Tear-of-the-Clouds, the summit water as I named it."

The Algonquins, Mohawks and other people of native America undoubtedly found the pond centuries before Colvin. They likely felt it, drank it and walked its shores. The Mohawks knowingly called the Hudson River *Co-ha-ta-te-a*, interpreted as "Great River having Mountains beyond the (Cahoh) Cohoes Falls," or simply, "River from Beyond the Peaks."

When European settlers reached the New World, they called the river the Great North River of the New Netherlands, or "Rio de Montagne"

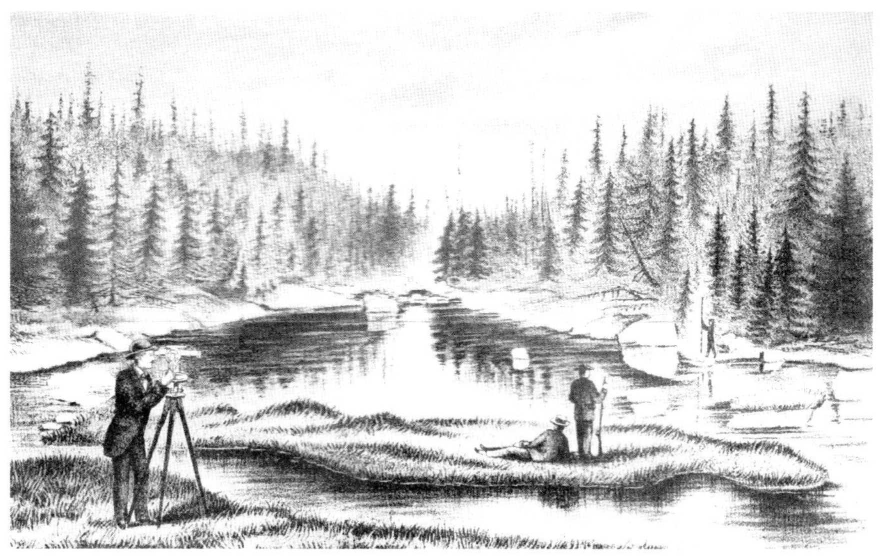

Lake Tear, circa 1879. *Sketch by Verplanck Colvin.*

(River of the Mountain). Eventually, Hudson River replaced the descriptive names that had paid tribute to the river's source. Yet explorers still sought the source. It was one of the most coveted discoveries in New York State.

As far as we know, Colvin and his guide, William Nye of North Elba, were the first white men to visit Lake Tear. Guides and tourists had reportedly looked at the little pond from the top of Mount Marcy and presumed that the outlet flowed east to the Ausable River. No one bothered to explore further until Colvin came to the region. He was curious about everything. So he ventured down the side of Marcy, up to the top of Gray Mountain and then down to the little pond. Surveying the area, he was able to determine that the pond did not flow to the Ausable but rather to the Hudson.

Just three years later, legendary guide Orson "Old Mountain" Phelps, with his son, Ed, and L.J. Lamb, had the honor of building the first trail to Lake Tear. But Phelps wanted more accolades, claiming he had earlier named the pond Lake Perkins in honor of artist Frederick S. Perkins. He criticized Colvin's "namby-pamby" name. However, others adored the name Lake Tear of the Clouds, thinking it was the aboriginal name for the pond.

Colvin originally called the pond Summit Water in his report to the state legislators. But he also described it as "a minute, unpretending tear of the clouds—as it were—a lonely pool, shivering in the breezes of the mountains, and sending its limpid surplus through Feldspar Brook to the Opalescent

River, the well-spring of the Hudson." When the statesmen read the report, they liked Colvin's poetic phrase and gave the name Lake Tear of the Clouds to the little lake.

As I look at the lofty pool nestled between mountain peaks, Colvin's words about these wild headwaters come to mind: "From the loftiest lakelet of New York the water descends, gathering volume at every brook, till in full breadth it swells before the wharves and piers of the metropolis, floating the richly burdened ships of all the nations."

Along its 315-mile journey, the Hudson River flows past the places where more than eight million people live, work and play. The river is, and always has been, an important commercial and recreational waterway, reflected in its designation as an American Heritage River in 1998. Organizations cooperate to promote economic development, environmental protection and historic and cultural preservation along the river's entire course, from the Verrazano Narrows in New York Harbor to Lake Tear in the Adirondack High Peaks.

As I get ready to make the return trek, and before the highborn water of Lake Tear can escape to the harbor, I capture a cupful and pump it through a filter. I swish the cool, clear liquid in my mouth and then swallow. Ahhh, life is good.

Passed By

Exploring a Forgotten High Peaks Route

I struggle through thick brush for an hour, unable to see my hiking boots or more than ten feet beyond my scratched forehead. Balsam needles dribble down my neck while more sift into my socks. Finally, I burst into open forest, only to find my next challenge: moss-covered boulders and rotted wood interspersed with holes large enough to hide caribou.

My hiking partner, Peter Biesemeyer, and I hadn't expected such obstacles that warm late-summer morning when we began our excursion. From Adirondak Loj, it had been a pleasant two-mile stroll to Marcy Dam. The misty view to the south charmed my eyes. The white slides of Mount Colden fell into the crevasse of Avalanche Pass. The dark green crown of Avalanche (once called Caribou) Mountain rose into open sky; its shoulder dipped down into a shallow notch and then ascended to Algonquin Peak.

That remote notch is labeled Caribou Pass on my 1979 USGS topographic map. Long ago, a hiking trail ran through the pass, and later there was a logging road. Today, moss, brush and trees hide the old paths. The only way

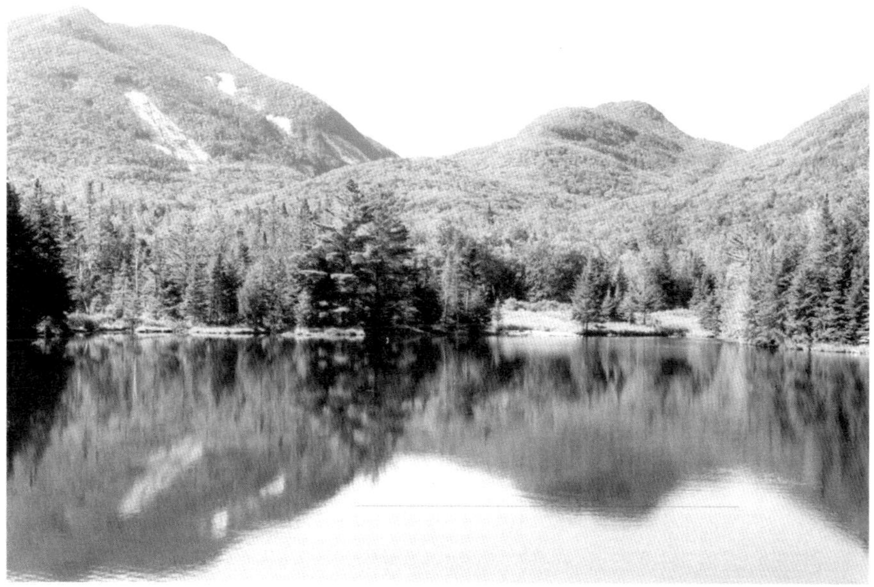

Caribou Pass from Marcy Dam.

to traverse the pass is to bushwhack: follow a mountain brook through the woods for two miles and climb more than one thousand feet in elevation.

That was our plan, anyway. From Marcy Dam, we hiked the Avalanche Pass trail, searching for the suitable place to veer across Marcy Brook. After two false starts, we located the fork in the stream and the old campsite that marked the beginning of our bushwhack. Luckily, deer paths and remnants of the old brook-side logging road made for agreeable hiking.

Peter showed me goldthread and blooming turtleheads as we meandered among the quiet woods. We contemplated how easy it would be to make this route a real trail. Then the road ended. We tried to follow the brook, but it was slow going through the thick brush that lined its course. We were still far from our goal—a four-acre meadow of blue-joint grass that lies near the southern end of the pass.

If we had wanted merely to visit the meadow, we could have come from the south, where the Algonquin trail runs within a few hundred feet. But we chose to traverse the pass. It was one of the few places Peter had never explored; I had my own reasons.

I had long suspected that there was an old route up Mount Marcy from the north. Henry Van Hoevenberg, builder of the original Adirondack Lodge, is credited with creating the first trail from the north in 1880. Prior to that, tourists trekked through Indian Pass to the deserted mining village of Adirondac and up the Opalescent River to Mount Marcy, a twenty-mile walk.

Mary MacKenzie, North Elba historian, shared my suspicion about a shorter route. She felt strongly that such a trail existed but cautioned, "You'll never be able to prove it." Searching old books, journals, diaries and maps, I found evidence: the trail did not go directly north off Mount Marcy but veered from the well-known Opalescent trail at Lake Colden and headed north to North Elba.

The first route navigated Avalanche Pass. An unpublished manuscript at the Adirondack Museum library, in Blue Mountain Lake, described guide Bill Nye leading a group along this path in 1867. The next year, Nye took Matilda Fielding up Marcy and through Avalanche Pass, christening the underwater shelves along the cliff walls "Hitch-Up Matildas."

In 1869, surveyor Verplanck Colvin marched his crew through the pass. He disliked the difficult route along the walls of Avalanche Pass, so in early September 1873, he explored the pass to the west. "Deep in the defile we were surprised to find a rich little oasis meadow of 'blue-joint' grass, which, thick and rank, rose to our elbows," he wrote. "It was full of paths made by deer, and cozy beds from which they had only risen at our approach. A discussion which ensued as we climbed the mountain side in regard to the American reindeer or caraboo [*sic*], was the occasion of our naming the new pass after an animal which once inhabited the region, but which is now, probably, here extinct."

No doubt, Colvin had been misled by hunters who claimed to have shot caribou in these mountains. But in 1893, the *Plattsburgh Sentinel* reprinted an article from *Forest and Stream* that stated: "Caribou probably never existed in the Adirondacks. No good authority for or evidence of their appearance in northern New York can be found." Elk, however, did live in the North Country until the 1830s, according to James DeKay in *Natural History of New York* (1842).

Regardless of the scientific findings, Colvin picked the name Caraboo Pass. He climbed to the top of the pass and measured its elevation: 3,662 feet above tide. Then his crew, which included Keene Valley guide "Old Mountain" Phelps, marched down the other side. Phelps maintained that Caribou Pass was higher than Avalanche Pass, "but a much easier way to get from Lake Colden to North Elba."

The year after Colvin's survey, the *Plattsburgh Republican* reported that a trail ran through the pass, and in 1876, "Caraboo Pass" appeared on the Essex County map. No matter how you spell it, this trail to Lake Colden and Mount Marcy clearly existed before the Van Hoevenberg trail.

However, Van Hoevenberg soon came along and improved the Avalanche Pass trail. Caribou Pass fell out of use until loggers began pushing their way up the mountain slopes in the early 1900s. According to mountaineer James Goodwin, a logging road existed from the Avalanche camp up to the top of the pass. A 1922 guidebook mentioned the "road into Cariboo Pass," but by the 1940s, only traces of the old lumbering road remained.

Second-growth forest is rapidly covering the scars of logging and thwarting modern-day explorers. I toil and sweat as I try to push through the prickly, intertwined branches. I see nowhere to go, but I go there anyway. Finally, the forest thins and the ground levels.

There is no marker, though I know I'm at the top of the pass. I have left behind the waters of the Ausable River and hence, the St. Lawrence. The next stream I see will flow south to the Opalescent, into the Hudson and ultimately to the Atlantic Ocean.

It is easy to see why author T. Morris Longstreth chose Caribou Pass as the sanctuary for the hero of his 1920 novel *Mac of Placid*. After a brawl with a mob of whiskey-soaked loggers, Mac hid in a cave at Caribou Pass. "The cave was a chance find of mine on a wild-bee hunt," he said, "and few others knew about it, as those who traveled the trails (meaning a dozen or so a year) preferred that through Avalanche Pass. A great slab of granite had fallen from a higher ledge and caught upon two boulders. With such portals and backed by the solid cliff it was impervious to all the elements, and roomy as you'd want." Eventually, Mac went back to town and won the girl. They married at Avalanche Pass, "in the presence of God and of His mountains," and lived happily ever after in the cave in Caribou Pass.

Ed and Grace Hudowalski explored the area in 1946. "Caribou Pass is not as spectacular as some of the other passes," wrote Ed. "It is, however, interesting and gives one a feeling of wild remoteness."

That is still precisely the essence of the route today—wild remoteness. No signs or sounds of humans. Hugged by mountain peaks, at the divide of the waters.

But we must descend. Down the slippery streambed we go. Then the brook drops underground, and we maneuver difficult but dazzling terrain. Everything is saturated with greenness. What isn't cloaked in moss is covered by green plants or olive green leaves or lime-colored algae—except the holes between the rocks, which are black and fifteen-feet deep.

I step, and my right leg plunges into space, my thigh wedged between a boulder and a root while my foot dangles in midair. I extricate myself and examine the damage; nothing is broken, only bruised and scraped.

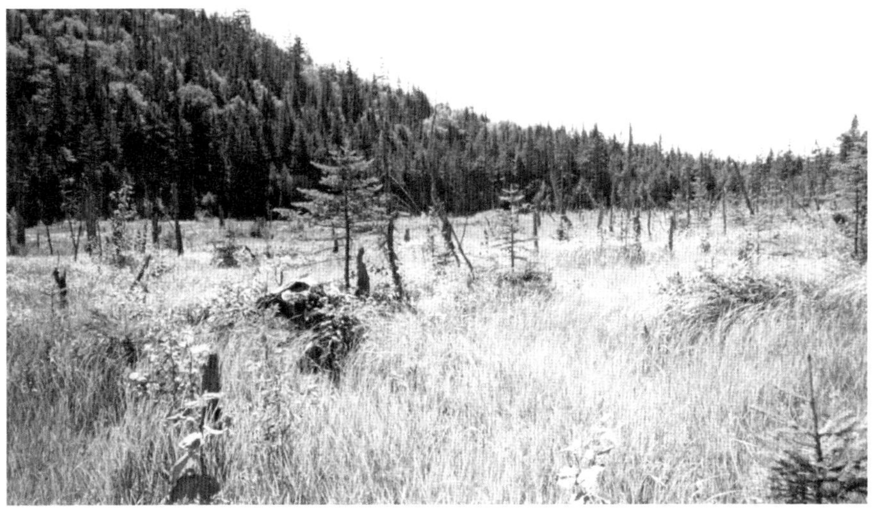

Meadow in Caribou Pass.

At last we come to level ground, and Peter spots two posts topped with the teeth marks of a beaver. Our meadow must be near.

And here it is, the first feeling of openness I've had in four hours. I inhale the sunlight and the sky, and the panorama of mountains, cliffs and forest. I wade through the waist-high grass, enjoying the soft muck beneath my feet and admiring the wild gentians. This is as fine a meadow as one can find in the Adirondacks.

As recently as 1982, people debated the merits of clearing a trail in Caribou Pass and removing the "Hitch-Up-Matilda" bridges in Avalanche Pass. Some hikers felt that the spans' metal substructures and pressure-treated decks were no longer compatible with their wild surroundings. Others feared that a trail built high in the pass would become a "new" bad trail. In the end, the structures remained; Caribou Pass stayed wild.

Peter and I return to Marcy Dam along the easier Avalanche Pass route. But I feel it was worth the effort to follow the footsteps of Colvin, Phelps and Mac through the old Caribou Pass route. Just once.

Making a Pass

Mountain passes offer a refreshing alternative to a steep climb up the surrounding peaks. They also offer choices: you can hike to the height of the pass and turn around; you can hike one way through the pass and have a second car waiting; or you can do a longer round trip by returning through a different pass.

All hikes, especially bushwhacks, require map-and-compass skills and route-finding experience. Carry a guidebook, a map, a compass, a flashlight with extra batteries, a first-aid kit and insect repellent, plus extra food and clothing. An altimeter is also helpful. Make sure you notify someone where you are going and when you expect to return; if there's a trail register, sign in and out. Have at least three people in your party.

CARIBOU PASS (between ten and eleven miles round trip depending on the return route): From Route 73, 3.0 miles southeast of Lake Placid, turn south on Adirondak Loj Road. The road ends at the Adirondack Mountain Club parking lot. From here, follow the Van Hoevenberg trail to Marcy Dam and the Avalanche Pass trail. Leave the Avalanche Pass trail at 2.7 miles, just before Kagel lean-to, which is out of sight near the brook. Enter the woods to the right and cross to the peninsula between the fork in the brooks. Head south along a herd path, which leads to an overgrown logging road. Follow the brook coming down from Caribou Pass until you reach the height of land at about thirty-six hundred feet. Descend, following a south-flowing brook, until you reach a meadow. Return via the same route or cross the meadow and follow the outlet to the Algonquin-Lake Colden trail. See the Keene Valley 7.5′ x 15′ topographic map.

AVALANCHE PASS (7.8 miles round trip): Follow the Van Hoevenberg trail 2.3 miles to Marcy Dam. Take the yellow Avalanche Pass trail to Avalanche lean-to at 3.3 miles. Continue on the yellow trail to the top of the pass at 3.9 miles. Mount Colden rises abruptly to the east, with Avalanche (Caribou) on the west. The pass contains debris from a 1999 landslide; the trail has been reestablished, but the flank of Mount Colden is still unstable. Keep moving.

INDIAN PASS (twelve miles round trip): From the ADK parking lot, follow the red trail around Heart Lake and then south. Reach Rocky Falls at 2.0 miles and Scott's Clearing lean-to at 3.8 miles. After a steep climb around boulders and up ladders, reach Summit Rock at 6.0 miles. Algonquin Peak rises to the east, and Wallface Mountain's thousand-foot cliff is opposite. Return or continue to Upper Works at 10.4 miles.

KLONDIKE NOTCH (6.3 miles one way to Johns Brook Lodge): This route slips between Yard and Howard Mountains and offers an unusual way to get to

Johns Brook Lodge (JBL). Turn south on Adirondak Loj Road. At 3.8 miles, park at the South Meadow Road junction. Walk along South Meadow Road for a mile until you reach the red-marked Klondike Notch trail. The Mr. Van ski trail crosses at a quarter mile. The height of land, a gain of 1,127 feet, is reached at 4.6 miles; JBL is at 6.3 miles.

Roosevelt's Ride

Vice-President Roosevelt started at 6 o'clock yesterday morning from the Tahawus Club with guides on a hunting trip through the forests. On receipt of the dispatches stating that President McKinley's condition was critical, men were immediately started in search of him. Up to 5 o'clock last evening it was impossible to locate him, but he was finally found on the top of Mount Marcy.
—New York Times, September 14, 1901

Theodore Roosevelt's affinity for the Adirondacks began when he was a boy. At Lake George, he played with a salamander and observed a hamster mouse and a bald eagle. Then he tried to ascend a mountain, but the climbing was so hard that he was "dead beat" before he came to the top. Near the Lower St. Regis, he was allowed to go "in the bush." He pitched tents, caught trout and listened to his father read *The Last of the Mohicans* by the light of the campfire. At Lake Placid, he helped collect one hundred species of lichens and fungi from a peninsula on the lake.

In 1877, at the age of eighteen, Roosevelt and Henry Minot, a Harvard classmate, published *The Summer Birds of the Adirondacks in Franklin County, N.Y.* Besides listing ninety-seven species, the book provided a glimpse of Roosevelt's intense interest in nature and the Adirondack wilderness.

Roosevelt moved on to political appointments, big game hunting in the West and rough riding up San Juan Hill. Yet it seems fitting that the Adirondacks—and the tallest mountain among them—provided the setting for one of the most exciting events in his life.

The story starts on September 6, 1901, with Vice President Roosevelt on an island in Lake Champlain, a stop on his way to the Adirondacks. He was speaking at an outing of the Vermont Fish and Game League at Isle la Motte when a telephone call came from the wife of the manager of the New England Telephone Company. She said that a story was coming in over the wires that President William McKinley had been shot at the Pan-American Exposition in Buffalo.

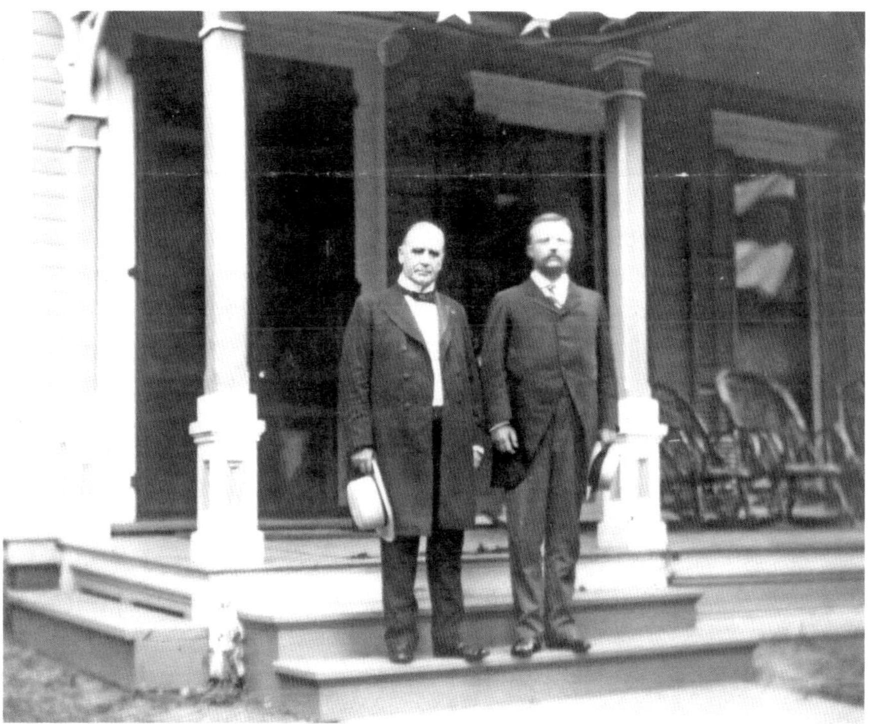

President William McKinley and Vice President Theodore Roosevelt, 1900. *Courtesy of the Library of Congress.*

Roosevelt boarded the yacht of Dr. W. Seward Webb and headed to Burlington. His friends warned him to avoid Buffalo because, as heir to the presidency, he might be in danger. Or he might appear ambitious and opportunistic. But not to go might appear insensitive. Roosevelt decided to do what seemed natural to him. He boarded a special train for Buffalo.

In Buffalo, he learned that the president's recovery was almost certain. He remained near the president, conferred with cabinet members and talked to the press. On Tuesday, September 10, after three days in Buffalo, Roosevelt announced to the press: "You may say that I am absolutely sure that the president will recover; so sure, in fact, that I leave here tonight."

Roosevelt and his private secretary, William Loeb Jr., left Buffalo. Loeb stayed in Albany to await further news, while Roosevelt went to the Adirondacks to join his family. Roosevelt's travel itinerary was kept quiet for fear there was a plot against his life.

On Wednesday, he arrived unannounced at the North Creek railroad station. The next twenty-five miles were over rutted country roads in an open buckboard. As if that were not enough, it started to rain. A drenched Roosevelt arrived at the Lower Works, the headquarters of the Tahawus Club (formed in 1897 as a successor to the Adirondack Club). Mrs. Edith Roosevelt met him, and together they rode another ten miles to a cottage at the Upper Works.

No doubt, Mr. Roosevelt asked about the health of Alice and Quentin, who had both been in the hospital recently. And Mrs. Roosevelt told him the exciting news: Theodore Jr. had just shot his first deer.

At the cottage, Alice, Theodore Jr., Kermit, Archie, Ethel and Quentin greeted their father. He probably added his wet clothes to the "shoes and stockings and little trousers and skirts, hung on lines in front of the fire to dry." As Mrs. Roosevelt put it, "The Adirondacks is probably the wettest place in the world."

Perhaps it is, but her children were only steps from the banks of the Hudson River, and as she said, "they did nothing but play there." Nothing, except sliding down the sloping roof of the cottage. Thankfully, she didn't know about that.

It seems that Roosevelt and the family had planned to leave the mountains on Friday or Saturday, but since the roads were bad from the storm, they decided to stay for several days. Besides, Roosevelt, the renowned woodsman,

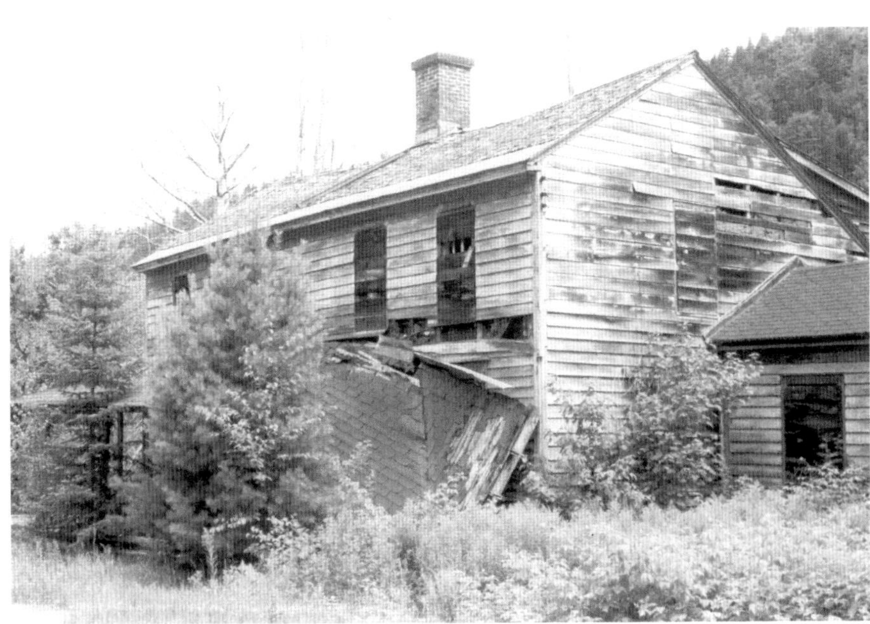

MacNaughton Cottage in 1999. The Roosevelt family stayed here in 1901.

declared that he wanted to climb Mount Marcy. He probably needed to escape the scrutiny and political pressure—and the criticism from some who said he seemed like a vulture at McKinley's bedside.

Apparently, Loeb was never informed of the change in plans. Of course, communications from Upper Works were not easy. The telegraph line came only to North Creek, thirty-five miles away. Telephone service was still quite rare in 1901. There were fewer than two million phones in the country. Yet a single-wire grounded telephone circuit connected North Creek with Lower Works. That telephone was still ten miles away—ten muddy, rutty, wretched miles away.

On Thursday afternoon, word reached Roosevelt that the president was in "splendid" condition. So the whole family, except four-year-old Quentin, set off for the woods. Miss Young, the governess; James MacNaughton, president of the Tahawus Club; two Harvard law students, Beverley and Herman Robinson; guide Noah LaCasse; and several other guides came along, too.

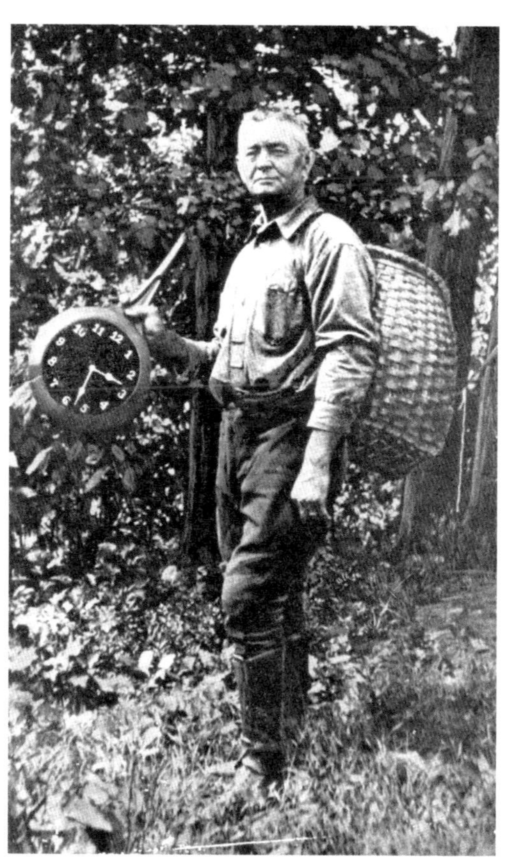

Guide Noah LaCasse with the frying pan clock given to him by President Roosevelt.

The large group walked five miles up the Calamity Brook trail to Flowed Land and then went by canoe to the western end of Lake Colden. They stayed overnight at two cabins, where they had "miserable little cots," slept on "balsam boughs" and rowed across the lakes to get to breakfast, according to Mrs. Roosevelt.

She may have had an uncomfortable night, but at least she was far from newsmen and assassins. Far from trains and phones. Far from the trouble in Buffalo. During the night, President McKinley's condition worsened. He was in great danger of dying.

Earlier reports had favorably construed his condition. The truth was that President McKinley "never had one chance to recover from the assassin's bullet." The surgeons had used all the resources of their science and their skill, but complications were beyond their control. They could not have detected the gangrenous infection.

Vice President Roosevelt had to be summoned quickly.

A telegram was sent to North Creek. It was relayed by telephone to the Lower Works and written down on a piece of paper. The paper was carried by buckboard and delivered to David Hunter at the Upper Works at a little after ten o'clock in the morning. Hunter called to the guides sitting around the fire at the clubhouse: "There is bad news from the president. Who will carry the message to Mr. Roosevelt?"

Tall, thin, fifty-three-year-old Harrison Hall was chosen. He quickly set off on the trail to Lake Colden. Along the way, he met Mrs. Roosevelt and the children returning to the cottage. Hall pushed on toward Mount Marcy and Roosevelt. But it was not easy.

"From the club to Lake Colden the path was plain and clear. Beyond there it had been rarely used, and the fallen deadwood clogged every step," reported the *New York Herald*.

> *Still, with the same sure, catlike stride, too wise to hurry, too eager to slacken speed, he pushed on through the black tangle of primeval forest. Many strange sights had those huge old gray pines beheld, many tragedies of hunter and hunted, but this spectacle of the silent messenger, with the fateful slips of yellow paper in his hand, was new to them. New also to the world, for never before had so strange a courier borne notice to a man of destiny that his time of ruling was at hand.*

Roosevelt and his companions were far ahead of the messenger. They had left Lake Colden at nine o'clock that morning and arrived at the summit about noon. Clouds loomed over the scene; it was not a good day for views. It was not a good day, period. It was Friday the Thirteenth.

Eventually, the sky cleared, and they could see far and wide. "Beautiful country, beautiful country!" Roosevelt said over and over. Then the sky darkened and heavy clouds rolled in. They quickly descended one thousand feet to Lake Tear of the Clouds and stopped for lunch.

Roosevelt started eating from a tin of ox tongue. "I was perfectly happy until I saw a runner some distance away," he later told a friend. "I had had a bully tramp and was looking forward to dinner with the interest only an appetite worked up in the woods gives you. When I saw the runner, I instinctively knew he had bad news, the worst news in the world."

Exactly what bad news was delivered and how Roosevelt reacted is unclear. In his autobiography, Roosevelt said, "He handed me a telegram saying that the President's condition was much worse and that I must come to Buffalo immediately."

Two accounts said that Hall handed the vice president a slip of paper that read, "The President appears to be dying and members of the cabinet think you should lose no time in coming." Another account said the message read, "Cortelyou wires President's condition causes gravest apprehension. Ansley Wilcox telephoned 6 a.m. slight improvement. Advise your coming here immediately. Will meet you if necessary. Will send special engine to bring you in case you miss the 10:20 train this morning." Roosevelt is reported to have said, "Complicated, complicated, it cannot be. I must return to the club at once."

Norman Hall presents a different version:

> *What happened next angered my grandfather, Harrison Hall. He had hurried as fast as the wet, slippery, foggy trail would permit any guide to travel. He knew the message he bore was urgent, and he had not even taken time to tell Mrs. Roosevelt about it when they met on the trail below. The Vice President took the message, read it, said nothing but calmly turned and finished his lunch. My grandfather never had much to say about that moment. It left him flabbergasted.*

Regardless of what was said, or not said, the party started down the mountain. Roosevelt reached the house about 5:30 p.m. and immediately asked if there were any further messages. No further word had come.

He decided he would not go to Buffalo right away. He sent a messenger to Lower Works to arrange for a relay of horses in case he needed them and to pick up any later messages. Mrs. Roosevelt reported that her husband told her, "I'm not going unless I am really needed. I have been there once and that shows how I feel. But I will not go to stand beside those people who are suffering and anxious. I'm going to wait here."

Surely, Roosevelt must have been tense wondering about the condition of the president. Of course, the entire country was tense, but for a different reason. They knew the president's condition; they knew he was dying. But they did not know the exact whereabouts of Vice President Roosevelt, and that was troublesome. They might have been even more troubled had they known that New York City detectives had just arrested a man who declared he was on his way to kill Roosevelt.

Throughout the afternoon and evening, Mike Breen at Lower Works took down various messages telephoned from North Creek—from McKinley's secretary, who reported on the poor condition of the president; from Secretary Loeb, who was on his way from Albany to North Creek with a special train; from various newspapermen requesting to accompany Roosevelt to Buffalo. Some of these messages were relayed to Roosevelt between ten and eleven o'clock that night. One of the messages stated that Roosevelt should come at once. Another said, "The President is dying."

Roosevelt threw on his clothes and jumped into a waiting buckboard. His friends argued that he should wait until morning; it was dangerous to go over dark mountain roads. He is reputed to have said that if they would not provide a rig, he would go on foot.

Dave Hunter hitched up a horse and wagon. "It had been raining a lot during the last few days and the road was in terrible shape," he recalled. "So we started out down through the mud—plunk, plunk, plunk." Amused by later news reports of breakneck speed, guide Ira Proctor said, "It was Jimmy Lindsay's big bay—must have weighed over 1,400 pounds. Of course he didn't poke along any, but he hardly broke a record."

At one o'clock in the morning, Hunter pulled the buckboard into the Lower Works. Roosevelt immediately went to the telephone. He called Loeb to say that he was on his way. Loeb told him the president was in a coma.

Roosevelt drank a cup of hot coffee and jumped into another wagon for the next nine-mile ride. Orrin Kellogg drove this leg of the relay through drizzle and rain. He gave Roosevelt his old raincoat to protect him from the mud splashing from the wheels. Unknown to either man, about halfway through the ride, McKinley died and Roosevelt became president.

Down the road at Aiden Lair Hotel, Mike Cronin waited and prepared to drive the next leg of the trip. Shortly before Roosevelt's arrival, a telegram from North Creek was telephoned to Cronin. The message said, "The President died at 2:15 this morning."

The people at Aiden Lair now knew they were waiting for the president of the United States. But Cronin asked them to keep the news a secret from Roosevelt. Why? "The astute driver thought it best not to increase his impatience or further try his nerves," reported the *New York Herald*.

When Roosevelt's wagon finally arrived at Aiden Lair at 3:15 a.m., very little was said. Roosevelt was urged to wait. He was told there were some bad spots in the road and it would be light in only a few hours. But Roosevelt wanted to push on. For him, it was still a race against death.

Cronin agreed to speed along the dark road, "keeping as tight a grip on his secret as he did on his reins." Cronin recalled, "At one place, while we were going down a slippery hill, one of the horses stumbled. It was a ticklish bit of road and I was beginning to get somewhat uneasy and began holding the team back, but Mr. Roosevelt said, 'Oh, that don't matter. Push ahead!'"

About two miles from North Creek, they halted. Roosevelt got out, stretched his legs and straightened his clothes. "To Mike Cronin, this was a treasured pause, as he watched his friend the President of the United States 'spruce up' for the occasion. Besides, those fleeting moments gave the horses the chance they needed 'to blow' before the last dash."

At dawn, the horses drew up beside the waiting train at North Creek. Cronin had covered the sixteen miles in one hour and forty-one minutes. He beat his own speed record by a quarter of an hour.

The excitement of Roosevelt's arrival was mixed with the graveness of the news that needed to be delivered. Cronin handed Loeb the slip of paper with the notice of McKinley's death. Loeb passed it to Roosevelt. Then the two men climbed aboard the train.

"As soon as Mr. Roosevelt was aboard, the engineer, with instructions to make the run of his life to Albany, pulled the throttle open and the train sprang out of the dawn into a stretch of track 104 miles long." However, the track was not clear. Two men on a handcar were on the track just north of Albany. Fortunately, the men jumped just a minute before the speeding train knocked the handcar off the track. Without further mishap, the train reached Albany shortly after eight o'clock. They changed engines and sped toward Buffalo, reaching there at 1:38 p.m. and "having broken every record for a run between Albany and that city."

Just past three thirty that afternoon, Roosevelt took the oath of office as the nation's twenty-sixth president. In one fast and furious gallop, he went from the summit of Mount Marcy to the highest office in the country. "It is a dreadful thing to come into the Presidency this way," he wrote to a friend, "but it would be a far worse thing to be morbid about it. Here is the task, and I have got to do it to the best of my ability; and that is all there is about it."

According to guide Noah LaCasse, the story does not end there. In a news interview, he said,

> *The man* [Mike Cronin] *that drove the last team of the three was also the proprietor of a resort hotel, where the rich and fashionable of the East gather yearly. And a half dozen times each year he has brought out a pair*

> *of horse shoes to show his guests, claiming that they were the original shoes on his team on that memorable occasion.*
>
> *The guests immediately suggest an auction and...the driver has since disposed of 25 pair of horse shoes at $25 a pair—all of which were the one and only "originals."*

Obviously, this was a tall tale, which grew taller with time. In 1960, author William Chapman White said there were four hundred "genuine" shoes.

The truth is that Cronin never sold horseshoes to anyone. But his wife says he did like a good story and perhaps had a hand in starting this tall tale.

Horseshoes are no longer required along the route from Upper Works to North Creek. The lower part is now Route 28N and designated the Roosevelt-Marcy Memorial Highway. A marker beside the macadam road marks the spot Roosevelt passed at 2:15 a.m. on September 14, 1901—the moment McKinley died.

In July 1999, a more permanent "marker" was designated in honor of Theodore Roosevelt. A 3,821-foot mountain located about two and a half miles north of Mount Marcy was officially named TR Mountain.

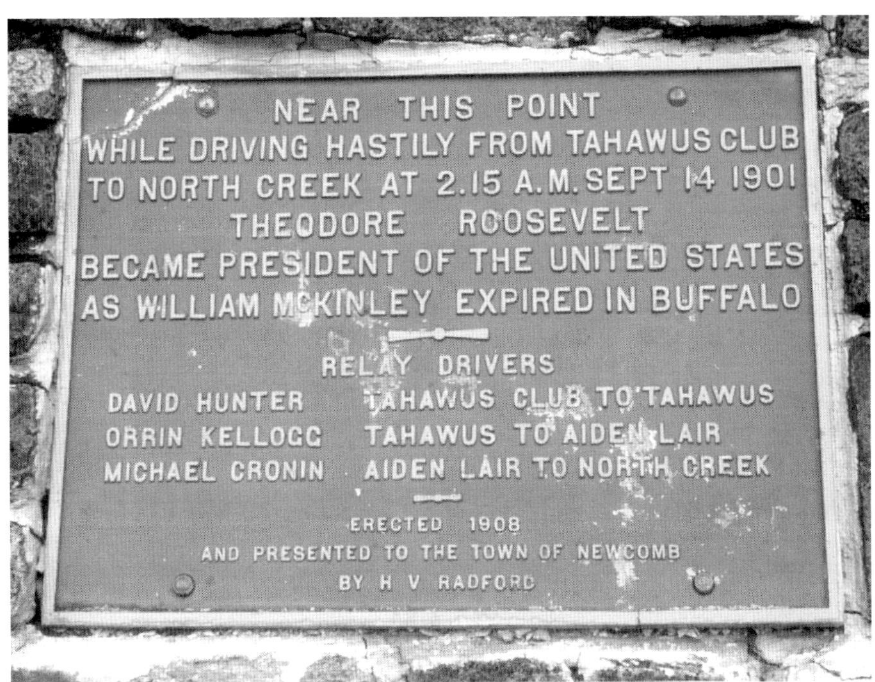

The plaque commemorating Roosevelt's ride from the Tahawus Club to North Creek.

Up Herbert Brook

It's a great thing these days to leave civilization for a while and return to nature.
—Bob Marshall (1901–1939), hiker and conservationist

Day 4, Saturday, August 2

Today we are climbing a mountain. The peak is 4,360 feet above sea level, and our camp is at 2,760 feet, so we will be going up 1,600 feet. That is not incredibly steep, since it is spread over a few miles. However, there are two snags. First, there is no marked trail; we will have to bushwhack. Second, rain and thunderstorms are predicted.

Despite all that, Marcy and I want to go. It will be a chance to hike without our heavy packs, and it will be our first climb up this peak, named for a great Adirondacker. Mount Marshall honors the life of Bob Marshall, one of the most important conservationists of the twentieth century. He worked for the United States Forest Service and fought to protect America's wild lands.

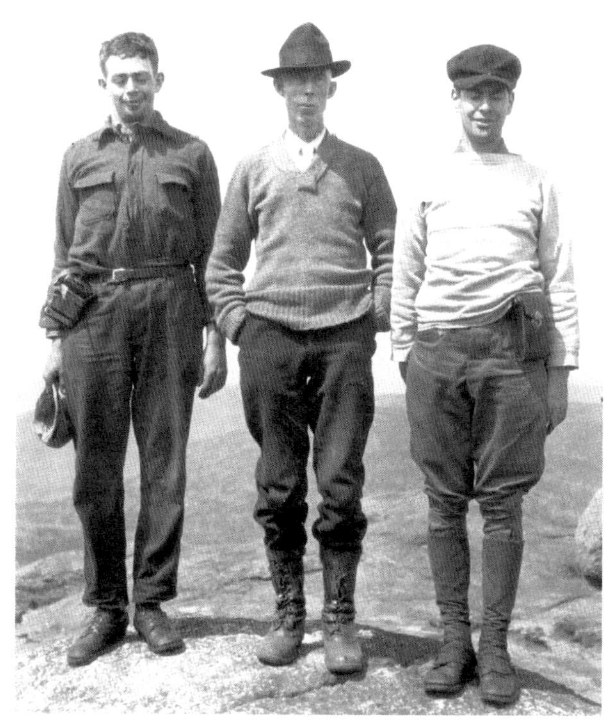

Bob Marshall, Herb Clark and George Marshall on the summit of Mount Marcy, about 1918. *Courtesy of the Adirondack Museum.*

Marshall hiked throughout the Rocky Mountains and Alaska, but his appreciation for wilderness started in the Adirondacks. In 1918, when he was seventeen, he decided to start climbing the tall mountains. His fourteen-year-old brother, George, came along, and so did forty-eight-year-old Herb Clark, who served as their guide.

Herb was an incredible mountain climber, especially when there was no trail to follow. He could sight a peak from a distant point and then walk for hours through the thick woods and emerge on the summit by the fastest and easiest route. At age fifty-one, he was still thought of as the fastest man in the pathless woods.

To keep the boys happy during their long walks, Herb loved to make up woods fables. He told one about a grandfather pickerel, which had gold teeth and spectacles, and another about Joe McGinnis, who had a disease that shrank him to the size of a baseball. The boys chuckled and walked, and soon they had climbed all the Adirondack peaks more than four thousand feet tall—a total of forty-six peaks. No one had ever done that. They were the first "Forty-Sixers."

Others followed in the footsteps of Herb, Bob and George, and eventually a club formed. The Adirondack Forty-Sixers now has more than five thousand members. The only requirement of membership is to climb all forty-six high peaks. (Recent measurements show that not all of the forty-six peaks are actually more than four thousand feet tall, but the club has kept the original list of peaks anyway.)

I have been working toward this goal for fifteen years. This will be my forty-first high peak. I hope to reach forty-six before the end of the summer. Marcy might climb all the high peaks someday, too. She has already climbed twenty-four.

Today's hike is extra exciting because we are joining a group of hikers, and among them will be Robyn and Jonathan, great-grandchildren of guide Herb Clark. We plan to climb Mount Marshall by following the Herbert Brook, which is named for Herb. It will feel as though he is guiding us, just as he guided Bob and George.

Despite the weather predictions, it is sunny as we begin our march into the woods and away from the hiking trail. Sometimes there is a deer path to follow. Sometimes we bushwhack through the trees. Most of the way, we follow Herbert Brook's streambed. It is a constant series of flumes and waterfalls tumbling over hard, smooth bedrock. Spongy moss and soft ferns line the banks.

Our shirts are wet with sweat, and our lungs are gasping for air when we reach the summit. Yet we raise our arms and shout the hikers' cheer: "We made it!"

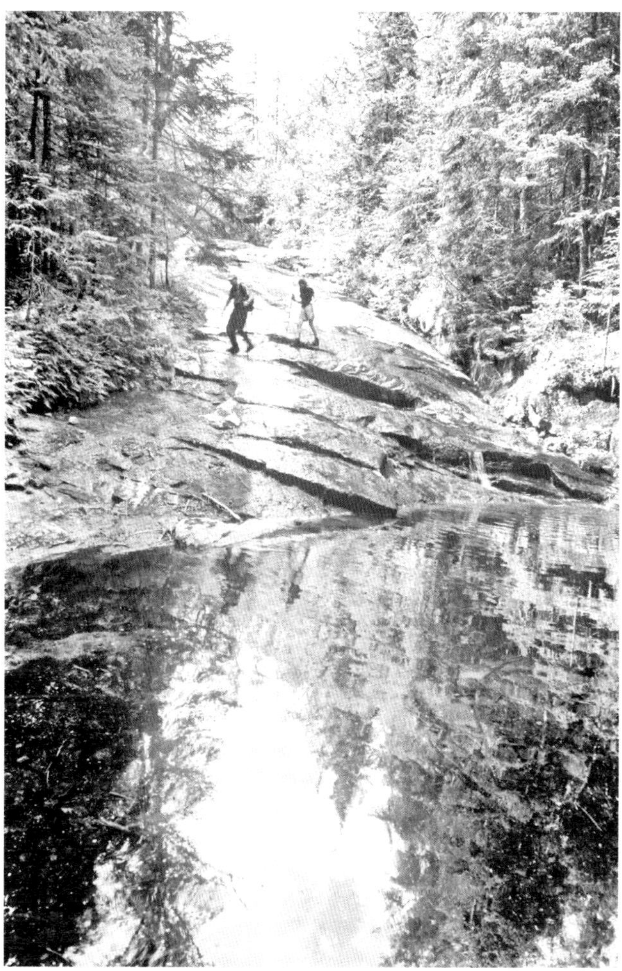

Following the streambed of Herbert Brook up the mountain. *Photo by Carl Heilman.*

The very top is covered with trees, so we do just as Herb, Bob and George did eighty-some years ago: we walk around and find ledges that jut out between the trees. The ledges offer surprisingly good views. From one, we look at the cliffs of Wallface, and from another we see a panorama of Flowed Land. We imagine the view is just as it was years ago. "This is probably the wildest mountain in the Adirondacks," wrote Bob Marshall in 1922. "In it all there was not a sign to show that man had ever been there."

After lunch, we head down the trail. It has been a good day of climbing.

Our friends keep walking toward their cars while we stay at our lean-to and cook dinner. At eight o'clock, we watch for the bear. There it is, right on schedule!

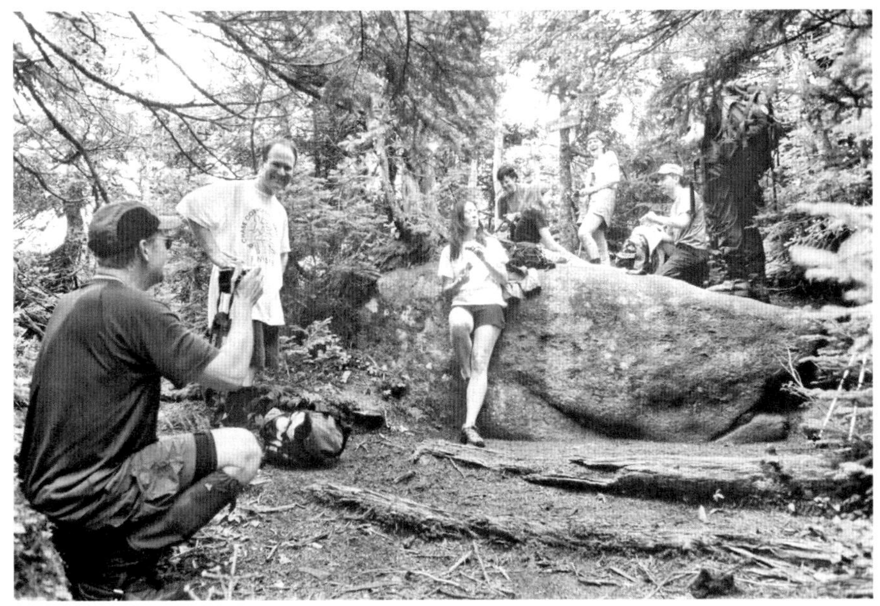

Hikers on the summit of Mount Marshall. Jonathan (standing, left) and Robyn (standing, center) are the great-grandchildren of guide Herb Clark. *Photo by Carl Heilman.*

It looks at us and we look at it. Looks like the same bear, and it probably thinks we look like the same campers—only dirtier and stinkier. Five long minutes go by before it finally goes over the hill. Then we hear the *thud, thud* of heavy footsteps on the hiking trail. The bear comes walking down the trail, crosses the brook and goes to visit other campers.

Marcy's Journal

Saturday, August 2

I didn't get much sleep. The bear came back three times during the night. He kept going to visit the campers across the brook, and they kept trying to chase him away.

They kept yelling, "Go away! Go away!" Finally, they got really mad and screamed at him, "You, BEAR, you! Don't you have anything better to do?"

Mom and I giggled.

Mountain Summits

A Foolish Adventure

Of all the stupid things I do, solo hiking is the stupidest. And the most stupendous. It is insensible yet sensible.

I face danger from injury, foul weather, erroneous trail markings, wildlife, dogs and humans. I face the horrific possibility of suffering frostbite or contracting giardia. I face the humiliation of getting lost and having to be rescued, becoming a statistic in the "Accident Report" in *Adirondac* magazine.

Still, I do it. I walk up a mountain. Step by step, mile after steeper mile, I climb over logs and rocks and squish through swamps. Absolutely alone. Without anyone to talk to or any sound of a car or radio or cappuccino machine. I hear only the thump of my own heartbeat.

At last, I reach the top, pause for breath and then go down. Mile after steep mile. Over logs and rocks and through swamps.

What have I to show for my toilsome effort?

Nothing whatsoever but stiff knees, scratched arms, muddy boots, a freckled nose and smelly armpits. Foolish indeed! Except for the experience of that brief moment on the top, in the hazy light, when I see the world as it was at the end of the last Ice Age. At my feet, I see mountain sandwort and Indian poke and blue-bead lilies. Over near the alpine bog, pink-flowered cranberry and dwarfed Labrador tea and tiny carnivorous sundews dwell.

This place is a virtual living museum of creatures from another world. Now that is something to see! But there is more. As I stand there, I listen to the reverberating silence. I imagine what the world was like before computers,

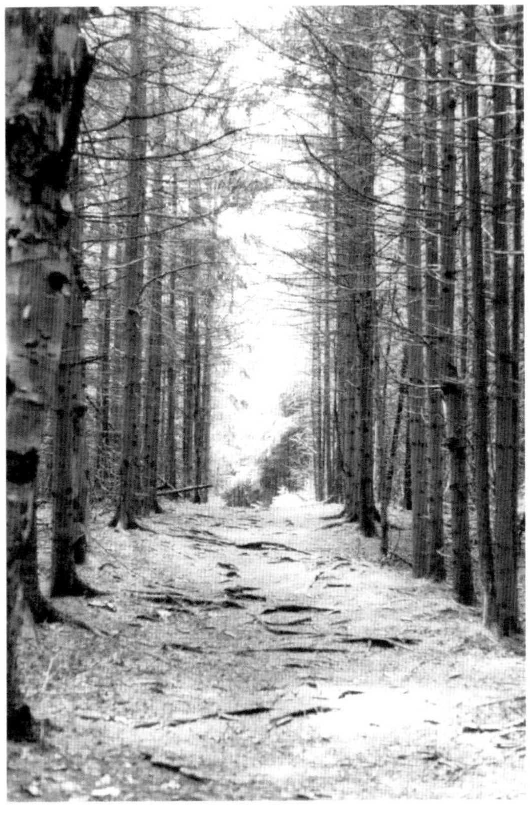

Along the trail to Marcy Dam.

cellphones, automobiles, chainsaws, fast food and Walmart. I dream a dream about uncivilized life, about wilderness.

I am alone with my thoughts—and the reindeer moss, nuthatch, lady's slipper, wood sorrel, fir, spruce, raven and hard gray rocks.

This is the reward of my foolish adventure.

I should be sated. Yet the very next day, I am ready to set off for the summit again. Why do I persist with such nonsense?

I have come to realize that the mountain is a symphony—a harmonious combination of elements. Elements of nature and man, of sight and sound and scent, creating a concert of classical compositions. I climb again and again because each time I experience some new facet or some new dimension. One day, I concentrate on the trees or the birds or the brook. Another day, I take notice of ferns or feldspar. Or there might be a rainbow, fresh snowflakes or unexpected cloud bursts.

Can I ever fully know every deep passage, every sweet note, every resonance?

Only if I take another foolish adventure.

Call It Tahawus

Before going one step further I must allude to what I deem the folly of a certain state geologist, in attempting to name the prominent peaks of the Adirondac Mountains after a brotherhood of living men. If he is to have his way in this matter, the beautiful name of Tahawus will be superseded by that of Marcy, and several of Tahawus' brethren are hereafter to be known as Mount Seward, Wright, and Young. Now if this business is not supremely ridiculous, I must confess that I do not know the meaning of the word. A pretty idea, indeed, to scatter to the winds the ancient poetry of the poor Indian, and perpetuate in its place the names of living politicians. For my part, I agree most decidedly with the older inhabitants of the Adirondac wilderness, who look with decided indifference upon the attempted usurpation of the geologist mentioned.

—*Charles Lanman, 1847*

This "name business" is "supremely ridiculous" but also titillating. It stirs sentiment and arouses passion. Reverend Joel Headley quipped that Mount Marcy, "as it is foolishly called," should be "properly Mount Tahawus." And

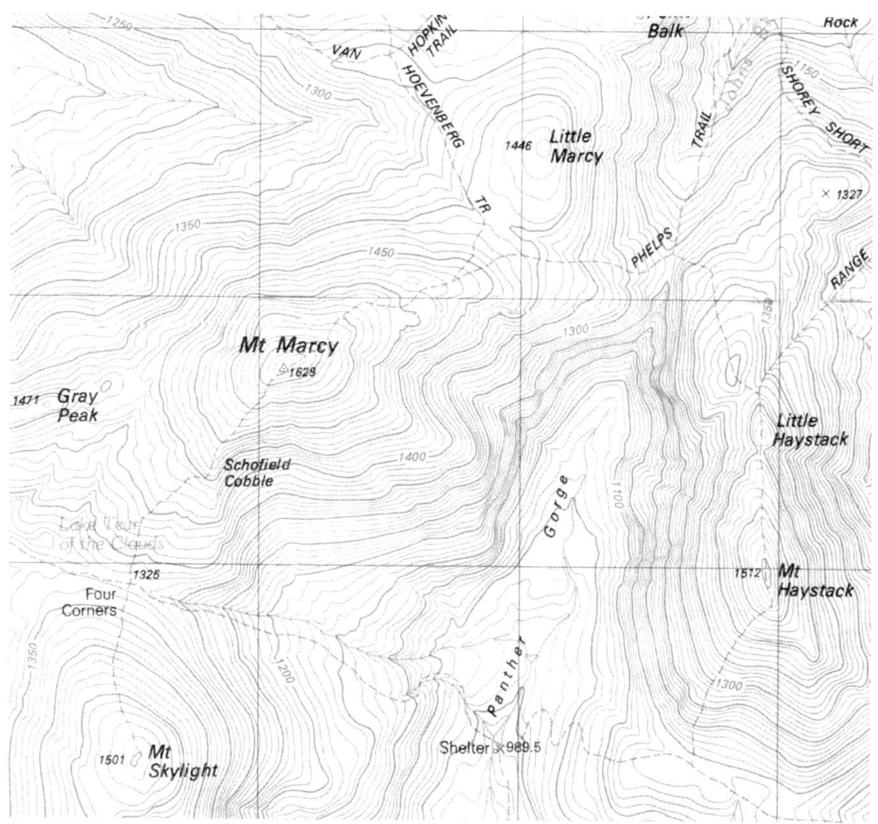

USGS map of the Mount Marcy area.

novelist Richard Henry Dana noted that it was "profanely called Mt. Marcy, by some sycophant of a state surveyor."

Such accusations and insults dictate that this ridiculous "name business" be addressed (by some sycophant of an author).

If Lanman's assertion that the peak was originally named Tahawus is correct, then the name Mount Marcy may be profane and foolish. But was the name Tahawus being "superseded" by that of Marcy? Was Tahawus an "ancient" name given by the local Indians?

No! It was a farce.

Poet and author Charles Fenno Hoffman visited the ironworks in September 1837, one month after the first ascent. He attempted to climb Mount Marcy, despite having an amputated leg. Guide John Cheney said Hoffman "would not be persuaded by words that he could not reach the summit; and when he finally discovered that this task was utterly beyond his accomplishment, his disappointment seemed to have no bounds."

Hoffman penned accounts of his trip, skillfully masking his failure to reach the summit of Marcy. In the *New York Mirror*, he wrote:

> *The highest peak…was measured during the last summer, and found to be nearly six thousand feet in height. Mount Marcy, as it has been christened, not improperly, after the publick* [sic] *functionary who first suggested the survey of this interesting region, presents a perfect pyramidal top, when viewed from Lake Sanford. The sharp cone was sheathed in snow on the day I took a swim in the lake; the woods around displayed as yet but few autumnal tints, and the deep verdure of the adjacent mountains set off the snowy peak in such high contrast, that soaring as it did far above them, and seeming to pierce, as it were, the blue sky which curtained them, the poetick* [sic] *Indian epithet of TAH-A-WUS,* He splits the sky, *was hardly extravagant to characterize its particular grandeur.*

This lovely last sentence caused widespread confusion. Since Hoffman was an authoritative Indian scholar and antiquarian, the public warmly received the name Tahawus and the picturesque translation, "Cloud-Splitter." It soon came to be believed that the mountain was originally named Tahawus and the foolish geologist Emmons had changed the name to Mount Marcy.

Possibly Hoffman did not intend this to happen. He did not suggest *naming* the mountain Tahawus; he simply evoked a poetic phrase and neglected to clarify its origin. But Hoffman should have been more astute. Surely, *he* understood the bewilderment concerning Indian names.

In an appendix to his poem "Vigil of Faith," Hoffman wrote, "It is very difficult even with the aid of the straggling Indians who still hunt the wilderness around the sources of the Hudson, to recover the aboriginal terminology… [T]he geographical names, therefore, often traceable to at least four languages, are necessarily much confused." Indeed, they are, Mr. Hoffman, and your inexactness has added to the confusion.

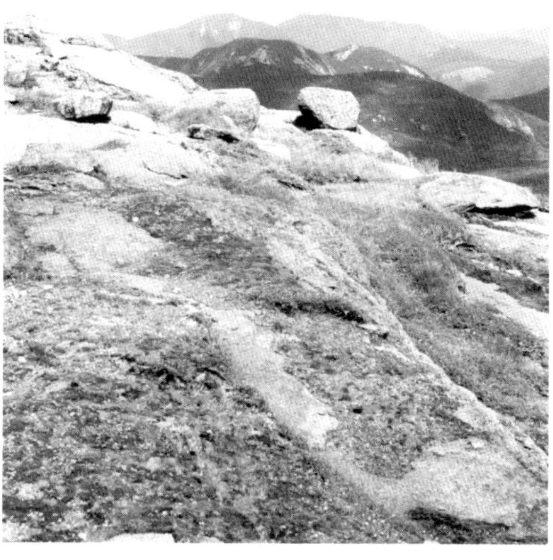

Summit of Mount Marcy.

It seems Hoffman never came forward to correct his oversight. Thus, in 1846, author Joel Headley popularized "Tahawus" in his articles. The name of the Lower Works was changed to Tahawus in 1847. And that same year, some mountaineers formed the Tahawian Association. To complete the contrivance, someone chiseled TAHAWUS into the rocks at the summit.

The nonsense was perpetuated because of growing public sentiment for Indian culture. According to Philip Terrie, professor of English and American culture studies at Bowling Green State University, the growing trend was to transform the image of the Eastern Indian from a devilish presence obstructing American civilization to a figure of myth and romance. Once the Eastern Indians no longer posed a real threat, they began to be romanticized and idealized. It was all part of an unconscious process of idealizing Indians, allowing whites to feel a bit less guilty for having stolen their land.

This sentiment was glaringly evident in author Wallace Bruce's argument for the use of the name Tahawus. He wrote, "There is no justice in robbing the Indian of his keen, poetic appreciation, by changing a name. We have stolen enough from this unfortunate race, to leave, at least, those names in our woodland vocabulary that chance to have a musical sound to our imported Saxon ears."

What an insensitive gesture Bruce made—names in exchange for land, wild game and a way of life. And who cares if they are authentic names so long as they are pretty names?

The overwhelming public support for the so-called "aboriginal" names squashed the truth-seekers. In 1865, Alfred Street wrote, "This name was either discovered or invented by that fine poet and profound Indian scholar and antiquarian, Charles F. Hoffman." An 1875 newspaper also reported that the aboriginal origin of Tahawus was "doubtful." Yet the supposed aboriginal name was firmly established, and as late as 1919, reputable organizations pronounced that "the Indians revered it as something sacred and they gave it the name Tahawus."

Finally, in 1921, the truth began to emerge. Alfred Donaldson, in *A History of the Adirondacks*, examined many of the "musical Indian names" in the region. He found that in nearly every case they were recent applications and seldom the names that natives used for the places. In regard to Tahawus, he wrote, "It was probably invented or first applied by Charles Fenno Hoffman, the versatile Indian scholar, who devised and compounded many another Indian name to meet the needs and whims of his poetic fancies."

A few years later, historian Russell Carson found that the name Tahawus was not from the local Abenaki. According to Mitchell Sabattis, "Mount Marcy in the language of the St. Francis tribe was known as Wah-um-de-neg, meaning that it was always white."

So where did the word Tahawus come from? "It is perfect Seneca," according to Dr. Arthur C. Parker, a full-blooded Seneca Indian and the state archaeologist in 1924. "Tahawus; he splits the sky," was listed in the 1827 book *Account of Sundry Missions Performed among the Senecas and Munsees; in a Series of Letters*. According to this book, it was not a place name but an abstract word of religion. Hoffman transplanted a picturesque Seneca name to Mount Marcy. "The ancient poetry of the poor Indian" was a farce. Hoffman, not the local Indians, was the first to apply the name Tahawus to the mountain.

As for the usurping of the name, all evidence points to the fact that the name Mount Marcy was given one month before Hoffman used the word Tahawus. Thus, the name Mount Marcy clearly preceded Tahawus.

But the widely read account of William Redfield obscured this fact. It referred to Mount Marcy as the High Peak of Essex. Redfield was on the summit when the peak was named, so why didn't he mention the name Mount Marcy?

Although Redfield said nothing publicly, he may have been miffed about the name. Years later, his son wrote, "Certainly it was hardly just that the explorer [Redfield]...should not have been honored by its name...At this day it is acknowledged that mountain summits should commemorate the names of scientists rather than those of politicians, or even statesmen."

Regardless, in 1837, Hoffman himself acknowledged that the name had been conferred, "not improperly," after the promoter of the survey. It seems he agreed with the reasons for naming the mountain in honor of Governor William Learned Marcy. Years later, surveyor Verplanck Colvin concurred, noting in his 1874 report:

> *The titles, Mt. Marcy, Mt. Seward and Mt. Dix, were given years ago by the State Geologists to the peaks which now bear those names...The titles of Mounts Marcy and Seward, though generally accepted, are objected to by many who prefer "cleaver of the clouds," and* Ou-kor-lah, *or the "great-eye." It seems appropriate, however, that we should have among our mountains, such majestic monuments to those who have so often received the public trust, and in that manner give a peculiar and historical character to our geography.*

However, by 1886, Colvin seems to have changed his mind and added to the name confusion. He used "the Marcy group" and "the McIntyre range" to refer to groups of peaks and supplanted the original summit names with "Mt. Tahawus" and "Mt. Algonquin."

In the 1920s, author Russell Carson was greatly disappointed to discover that Tahawus was not the original name and seemed to put forth the same ambiguity as Colvin. "Personally I like the name Tahawus best," wrote Carson. "But really it should make no difference for both names will always exist and we should not forget that Gov. Marcy, while not an Adirondacker, was the originator of the Emmon's [*sic*] survey which was the first great step in opening the Adirondacks to the people, and as such is worthy of such an honor."

Despite the intense historical research Carson conducted in his search for the truth, he allowed the name chaos to continue. In 1937, a plaque was erected to honor the centennial of the first ascent of the mountain. The top portion reads:

1837—Marcy—1937
also known by the Indian name
Tahawus meaning Cloud-Splitter

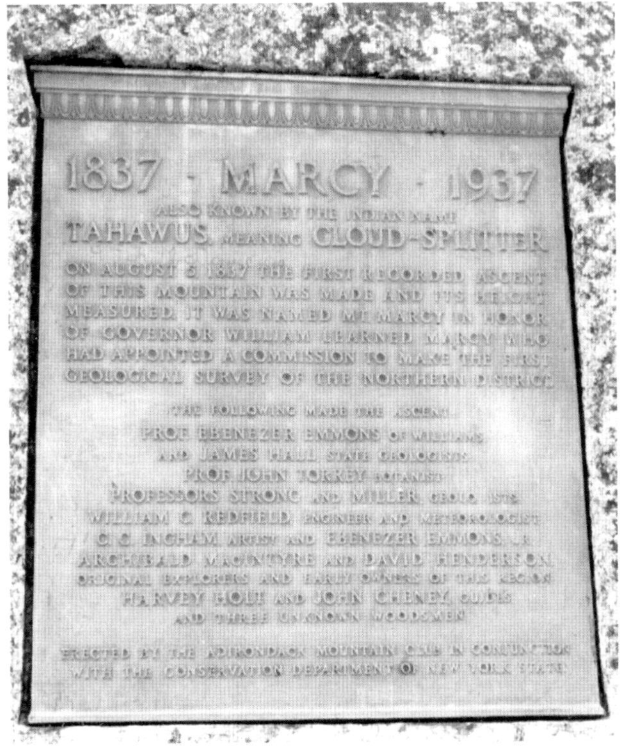

The plaque at the summit of Mount Marcy.

Of course, the words do not say that the Indians used to call the mountain Tahawus. But anyone might interpret it as such. And so, until the forces of nature wear away at man's bronze words, the mountain shall have two names, neither being an aboriginal name for the mountain. One bestows a fitting, poetic platitude, and the other honors a man responsible for its exploration.

PHONIC MOUNTAINEERS

No muscle-thumping mountaineer expects to climb the highest peak in New York and listen to poets recite verse. But that's exactly what happened to Mount Marcy hikers on July 27, 2002.

The United Nations General Assembly declared 2002 the International Year of Mountains, hoping to increase awareness of the global importance of mountain ecosystems. An organization called Dialogue Through Poetry decided to broadcast the message by holding poetry readings on the Seven Summits (the highest peaks on the seven continents) and other lower mountaintops.

In July, the chosen peak was Mount Marcy. While some of the poetic stanzas recited that day were new, the idea of such a celebration was old. Hikers stood on that summit as early as 1837 and celebrated the view, the rare alpine flowers and the August ice. No one recited poetry that day.

However, a decade later, in early August 1847, Dr. David P. Holton, superintendent of schools for Essex County, New York, held a different sort of celebration. He led a group who called themselves the "Phonic Mountaineers" to the summit of Mount Marcy. They read poems, sang songs and gave speeches and then engraved the New Phonetic Alphabet (devised by Dr. Andrew Comstock) into the summit rocks.

The Phonic Mountaineers had held a similar celebration atop Whiteface Mountain in July. In addition to reading poems and discussing phonetics, the group gave a hearty "discharge of vocal explosions of the elementary sounds of the English language." Before leaving, they carved phonetic characters into the mountaintop.

Records of these bizarre events were later discovered by C. Scott Brown and Levi Pond and publicized by Russell Carson and George Marshall. Marshall was surprised and disillusioned to learn that as early as 1847 the summit of Mount Marcy had been covered in "phonographic" characters. However, he writes that the text of the original account is unclear at this critical point, and "it looks as though the characters may have been 'pornographic.'"

Dr. Holton was an enthusiastic fan of Dr. Comstock, who had created his own version of phonetics intended to aid in teaching reading and improving speech. Holton not only read about phonetics and promoted their use but he was also gung-ho. On August 4, 1847, he conducted phonetic exercises at the Adirondack Iron Works, including his own lecture, "The Excellencies and Claims of the New Alphabet in the Schools of Both Heathen and Christian Lands." Others gave speeches, sang songs and read poems. Dr. Comstock read a poem that had been written at the request of Holton. "Comstock Phonetic Alphabet" praised the phonetic system, but according to Marshall, "it included one of the earliest descriptions in bad verse of the view from Tahawus [Mount Marcy]."

One of the verses went:

Ope thou the Phonians' portal, Truth devine!
We come to pay our vows at virtue's shrine:
We sacrifice upon the altar here.
The fallacies of time, which fools revere!
See yonder McIntyre, McMartin's peak,

Proud Santanoni, Henderson, and bleak
Mt. Boreas, and the Taylor Mountain grand.
Ranged round Tahawus which doth all Command!
Far North, soars Whiteface, by Lake Placid's shore.

We stand and look down on the Empire State!
Girt by the Clinton range which doth await
Upon Tahawus; We rejoice to see
Our mountain mid his giant family.
Explode the elements of our nervous speech
Which all the tongues of man combine t'enrich!

Ring out the Saxon consonated cry
And let the iron-echoed crags reply.

When the exercises ended, Holton and some of the attendees ascended Mount Marcy. They resumed the poetry reading, singing and lecturing. At the end of the celebration, they carved the phonetic alphabet into the summit rock. But that was not the end of this frenzied carving business.

On October 18, 1847, the Tahawian Association, with Holton as secretary, held its first meeting at the Essex County Courthouse in Elizabethtown. They proposed building a fifty-mile "pedestrian road" that would go from Keene Valley to the summit of Mount Marcy, down to the ironworks, northward through Indian Pass to Lake Placid, eastward to the top of Whiteface and down to Wilmington. A fund was established to prepare the road and to hold an "educational convention" on Mount Marcy in August 1848.

Their plan for the trail was grandiose but worthwhile. And the plan for more phonetic poems and speeches was frivolous but harmless. However, there was another plan. The first resolution of the meeting stated that all of those who gave at least one dollar or worked on the road for two days would have their names engraved on the summit of Mount Marcy.

It is hard to believe that such an unseemly scheme was ever contrived, much less approved, by the Tahawian Association. These men were not misfits or radicals; the list of officers reads like a who's who of Adirondackers: Archibald McIntyre, Orlando Kellogg, A.C. Hand, Monroe Hall, Charles B. Hatch, Wendell Lansing, Byron Pond and others. Fortunately, the association dissolved, and the plans were never executed.

In 1849, guide "Old Mountain" Phelps reported that the phonetic characters carved in 1847 were still clearly visible. He also said that someone had re-cut them to a depth of three-quarters of an inch "for fun!" By 1877, the characters had been "erased by weather," according to Phelps.

Thankfully, today's Phonic Mountaineers do not cut letters into the summit. They are content with the pleasure of letting their poetic stanzas ring out across the echoing iron crags.

Who Was Jo?

The love story of Jo and "Mr. Van" reveals how the High Peaks' most famous low peak got its name.

Whenever I visit Adirondak Loj, I can't resist walking along the shore of Heart Lake and up the slopes of Mount Jo. The short hike to the rocky, open summit of Mount Jo always rewards me with a magnificent scene. While my eyes peruse the panorama, my mind wanders and wonders about this woman Jo. Why was she honored on this glorious little mountain? Who was she? And what became of her?

After a few years of digging and hunting, I found that, like the mountain, the short story about the namesake Jo rewarded me with a magnificent

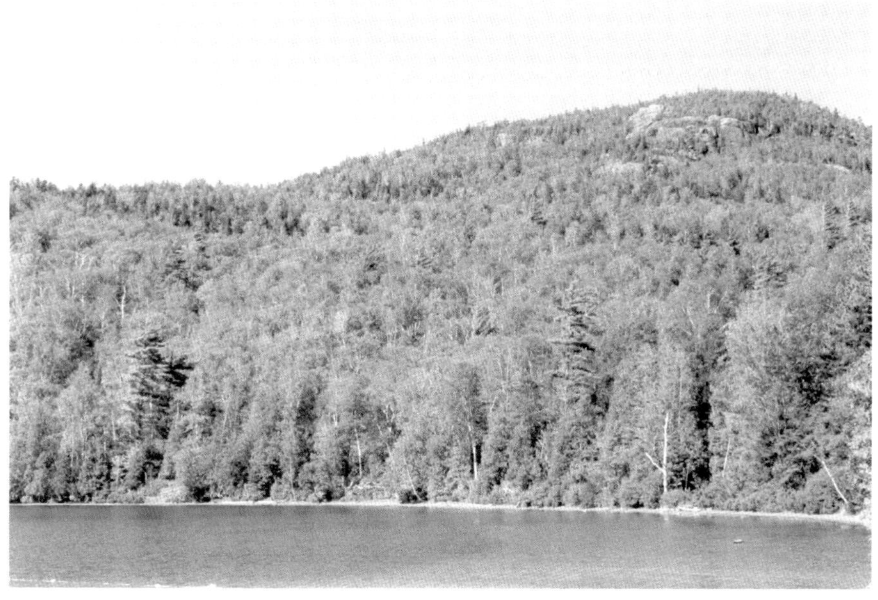

View of Mount Jo from Heart Lake.

drama. The story begins years and years ago—fifty years before the present Adirondak Loj took shape—in the days of stagecoaches, primeval forests and everlasting love.

In 1877, Henry Van Hoevenberg, the man affectionately known as "Mr. Van," first ventured to the Adirondack Mountains. He soon became well known as the builder and innkeeper of the enormous rustic Adirondack Lodge at Clear Pond (now Heart Lake). Much of the success and fame of the lodge owed to the romantic mystique surrounding the reason Henry built this artistic log house.

What happened in 1877 to inspire Henry, a successful electrician and inventor, to build the lodge? Alfred Donaldson recounted the popular story in *A History of the Adirondacks* (1921):

> *The building of Adirondack Lodge traces back to romantic beginnings. Mr. Van's first visit to the mountains was in 1877 when, with some friends, he camped on Upper Ausable Lake. In the party was a Miss Josephine Scofield, to whom he became engaged. The young lovers were naturally under the spell of the Adirondacks, and wove them ardently into their plans for the future. They decided to climb the highest mountain and from its summit select the most beautiful spot in sight as the location for a future home—a home that was also to be a house of entertainment for friends and acquaintances.*

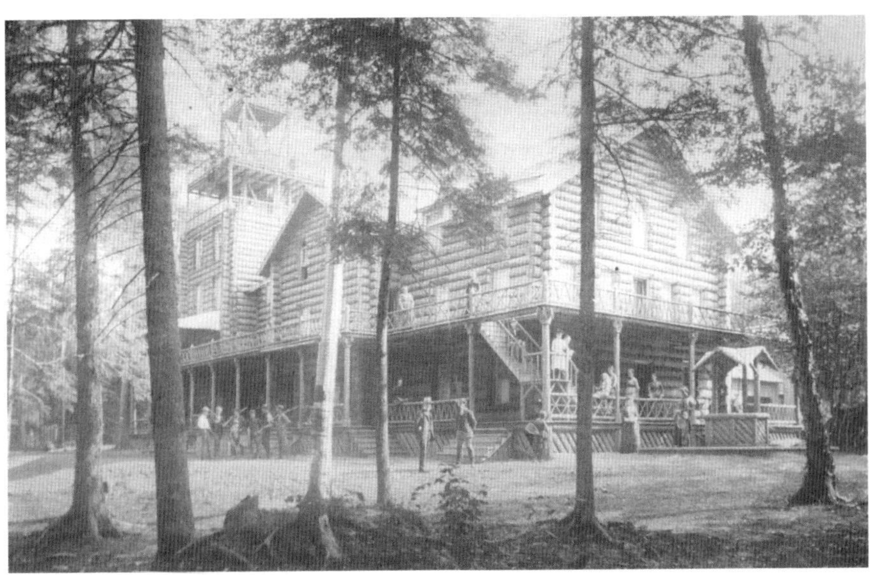

Adirondack Lodge, burned in 1903.

> *They ascended Mount Marcy, and found in the outlook some embarrassment of beautiful spots. Finally, however, they agreed upon one. It was a tiny lake that looked to them like a heart-shaped sapphire deeply cushioned in the velvety green of primeval tree-tops. It lay in utter seclusion, the mountains rising sheer from its shores. One of them was immediately named Mount Jo, in honor of Miss Scofield. The spot she chose became the site of the lodge, but she did not live to see it built. She died suddenly within the year.*

What Really Happened?

Ever since, people have talked and written about Henry Van Hoevenberg's tragic love affair with a Brooklyn girl named Josephine Schofield (the correct spelling, unlike Donaldson's). It is one of the most fantastic and romantic tales from the Adirondacks, yet the particulars are unauthenticated. Various versions of the incident have been put forth, including the sensational version best told by Eleanor Early:

> *You'd think that Miss Jo's father would have been glad for her to live in such a wonderful castle with a man as worshipful as Mr. Van. But Mr. Scofield had other plans. He wanted Jo to marry a friend of his. And when she refused, he ramped and stomped like Mr. Barrett of Wimpole Street. And Jo was so heartbroken that she did an irrevocable thing. She jumped into Niagara Falls.*
>
> *Descendants of Mr. Van Hoevenberg deny that there is any historical basis for this sad and romantic story, but I have found it in the accounts of the times, and so it must be true. The descendants say that "the affection between the two did not mature into the hoped-for marriage, and Miss Scofield died a sudden and untimely death."*

It's a great story—sweet romance and sad tragedy set in the wilderness. But it is just a story. Could the idea that Josephine jumped over Niagara Falls, as incredible and preposterous as it seems, be true?

Lake Placid Club secretary Harry Wade Hicks later vehemently denied the story, saying, "Extensive correspondence proves this story is fiction. The girl did not commit suicide but returned to her home in Brooklyn." He had, however, said in an earlier article, "It is true that her death was sudden—within a year."

Significant evidence to support the Niagara Falls story comes from two obscure sources, both written by wealthy, educated, refined women. Helen

Bartlett Bridgman was a book and newspaper writer and wife of Herbert Bridgman, a business manager, explorer, scientist and the man to whom Admiral Peary cabled the famous message: "Sun." Mrs. Bridgman visited the lodge several times, was guided by Henry on hikes and seems to have come to know him quite personally. She wrote about Josephine's actions:

> *Out of the heavily falling rain there rose before me the noble form of Mount Jo, bearing forever the name of her whom he loved well; of her who preferred death to separation from him—torn as she was between a stern paternal will and her heart's desire.*
>
> *How could the Lady Josephine, being first of all a woman, ask for a better fate than this: to be enshrined eternally in one faithful heart—to be known for all time through a changeless mountain? Though her body was whirled in the maw of Niagara to some bleak unknown, her soul must dwell about that sacred spot in a vast peace.*

Stranger than Truth

The second account is written by Julien Gordon, the pen name of Mrs. Julie Grinnell Storrow Van Rensselaer Cruger. She was the grandniece of Washington Irving, the wealthy widow of Colonel Van Rensselaer Cruger and the author of several successful novels and magazine articles. One article is described in the *Adirondack Bibliography* as a "romance based on the life of Henry Van Hoevenberg."

The article, titled "Underbrush," appeared in the magazine the *Smart Set* in September 1901. Mrs. Cruger described a visit to the mountains, where she decided to go to a "quaint tryst of hunters" run by a man who had a "pronounced reputation for refinement." Her host, "Mr. Ingen," was a "little man" who wore a "rough leather suit and leggings."

The following is a condensed version of the story:

> *Two days after she arrived, Mrs. Cruger found herself alone with Mr. Ingen, the "autocrat of the underbrush." The other guests had gone to spend the chilly night in their rooms. The two stood on the porch overlooking the bonfire in the road below. Mrs. Cruger recalled:*
>
> *"For an hour of life our souls understood each other, and I am ingenious enough to believe that he did not tell his story often; nay, I will even go so far as to say that it did not have the ring of an oft-repeated experience. It was rather wrung from him by my eager and earnest sympathy."*

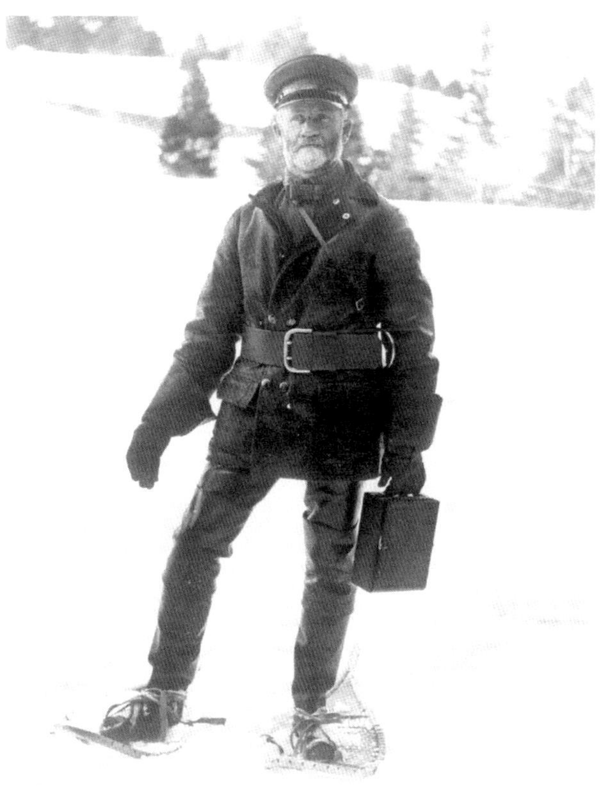

Henry Van Hoevenberg, known as "Mr. Van," dressed in one of his leather suits.

Ingen explained that he and his sweetheart were never engaged. He had never known her or her family; she was Canadian. Ingen had met her on a camping trip and thought her to be very talented and beautiful, even a goddess or Madonna.

One day they wandered together through the mountains and through his glass they spied a little lake in the wilderness. Ingen said:

"She fancied it. We sat down on a ledge of rock and planned…this house. How we would build it near the water, all of logs, with wings and turrets just as it stands to-day, and laughingly she told me we should live here, away from all the world. It was only for fun, you see, because when I asked her hand two weeks later she told me she was engaged to another man; that she disliked him, but that he was rich and her father desired she should marry him.

"…She was trained to obedience. She dared not flout him. She told me he was strong and severe, but I think he must have been very weak. It is only weak men who torture women; they like to show their power; strong ones with intelligence use it in other channels."

Thus they parted. But Ingen could not live without her: "I heard she was stopping with some relatives in Boston. I went there; she had just left them. Two days later I read of her in the papers. It made some noise at the time. On her way back to Toronto she went to the Falls. She was last seen on Goat Island. They found her hat and book."

Ingen did not know why she disappeared at Niagara Falls. He did not know if she loved him. Ingen scraped together all the money he could and went back to that spot in the Adirondacks. He bought the mountain and gave it her name. Then he bought the lake, opened a road, and built the house they had planned together.

"I lived here alone and was happy, after a fashion...those who look for anything more than amusement in society will find disappointment. I chose solitude. I am content.

"...I don't care for money; I hate it. It killed my poor love. I have lived here twenty years; she was...lost on September 14, 1876. To me it seems but yesterday, and yet it is twenty years."

Ingen thought of building a marble mausoleum for his lady but feared the intruders and tourists. Still it saddened him that her beautiful, dear body was never found and she had no burial place. "The mountain is her monument," he said.

Wealth of Evidence

That is the essence of the fictional "Underbrush" account. Clearly, "Mr. Ingen" was a disguise for "Mr. Van." Cruger's "quaint tryst of hunters" and "autocrat of the underbrush" are synonymous with Adirondack Lodge and Henry Van Hoevenberg.

The most astounding part of the "Underbrush" story regards Ingen's lady. She was Canadian, engaged to a rich man, and met her death at Niagara Falls. Was this lady "Josephine Schofield"? A wealth of evidence confirms that a Canadian woman, who was engaged to a Toronto businessman, disappeared (and likely committed suicide) at Niagara Falls. Her name was Miss J.J. Schofield.

A *New York Times* article of October 22, 1877, titled "The Suicide at Niagara Falls," reported the disappearance and presumed death of Miss Schofield. The young lady, said the *Times*, had grown up in Woodstock, Ontario, and was proficient in telegraphy and also well known as a contributor to magazines. "Some few months ago she had to give up her position owing to illness, and has since been staying at Staten Island, New York State, for the benefit of her health. She was on her way home when the melancholy occurrence took place."

Miss Schofield apparently jumped over Niagara Falls on October 15, 1877. (This was exactly one year, one month and one day later than the date given for the lady's jump over Niagara Falls in the "Underbrush" story.) The newspapers reported her name as Jane, J.J. and Jennie J. Schofield and noted that she had traveled to the Adirondacks recently.

As a young woman, Jane worked as a telegraph operator for the Dominion Telegraph Company in Woodstock, Ontario, Canada. She acquired such skill that she was appointed to the position of amanuensis (shorthand writer) in the company offices in Toronto. Evidently, her talents also caught the attention of a prominent professional man. Charles A. Kelly, a bookkeeper and coppersmith, planned to marry Jane in the fall of 1877.

Unfortunately, 1877 was a terrible year for the Schofield family. On April 13, Jane's younger brother, Frank, died of consumption, which was incurable at the time. On July 5, her sister, Hannah, died after struggling with the same disease for six months. Then Jane took ill.

About August 1, Jane left her job and went to Staten Island, New York, where she accepted a position at a branch office of the Western Union Telegraph Company. When that office closed, she was appointed shorthand writer in an office in New York.

While in New York, Jane was under medical treatment for her premonitory symptoms of consumption. It is likely that she felt very desperate by the end of the summer and so decided to travel to the Adirondacks to seek relief. In all likelihood, Jane (Jennie) J. is the Miss Schofield who joined Henry Van Hoevenberg and his party camping out at Ausable Lakes. It seems she used the name Josephine or Jo while in the Adirondacks. Presumably, her middle initial, "J," stood for Josephine, although there is no document to certify it. It is possible she had been using the name Josephine or Jo for quite some time; perhaps it was her pen name.

At the end of two weeks, Jane's health had improved in the mountain air, and it appears that she returned to New York City, where she was in good health for some time. The *Niagara Falls Gazette* reported, "[She] appeared to be still further improved in health, until she imprudently ventured out and caught cold, which settled in her lungs, and necessitated imperative orders from her physician to return home."

Jane boarded a train in New York City on Monday, October 15. She was traveling to Toronto but decided to stop over in Niagara Falls. Jane had arrived at Buffalo and registered at the Tift House Hotel as Miss J.J. Schofield.

At 6:00 p.m. she boarded a train for Niagara Falls, arriving there at 7:00 p.m. She telegraphed Mr. Kelly, "Trains do not connect. Can't get home tonight. Am going crazy." She noticed the telegraph operator observing her ill appearance and strange behavior and remarked that she had "neuralgia in the head so bad that it seemed as though she would go crazy."

At 7:30 p.m., she walked out to Goat Island, telling the man at the gate that she was "an artist, and wished to see the falls by moonlight." The tall young lady dressed in black was never seen again.

The reason for her suicide might have been her illness. Perhaps her helplessness and bleak outlook were compounded by her relationship with Henry Van Hoevenberg. She had met a man of similar interests in telegraphy and writing and nature. She had spent two weeks tramping and talking and dreaming with him in the Adirondack mountains. She had spent two weeks free of illness, father and fiancé and likely dreaded returning to those confinements. We will never know what was in her heart.

Henry Van Hoevenberg, the man Jane (Josephine) met in the Adirondacks, was never able to forget her. He remained a bachelor. He spent years building a memorial to her and lived the rest of his life near Mount Jo. The term "jo" means "sweetheart, darling, dear." This offers an intriguing possibility for why the mountain is called Mount Jo, although the lady was named Jane: Henry's sweetheart was Jane. He called her, and the mountain that memorializes her, Jo.

MOUNT VAN HOEVENBERG

Brittle blue that mile long
paleolithic serpent
half-way bulged at SHADY
digesting sleds and sliders.
—Margaret Roy, World Cup, Mount Van Hoevenberg, February 1987

In 1904, the teenager Godfrey Dewey and veteran woodsman Henry Van Hoevenberg had great fun frolicking together in the snow and ice at the Lake Placid Club. These two friends and eight other participants did not realize that they had just made Lake Placid the first winter sports resort in America.

It was later observed, "For too long in the United States winter meant a cessation of outdoor activity and the undoing of most of the benefits gained from an outdoor life in the summer. Today, largely because of the efforts

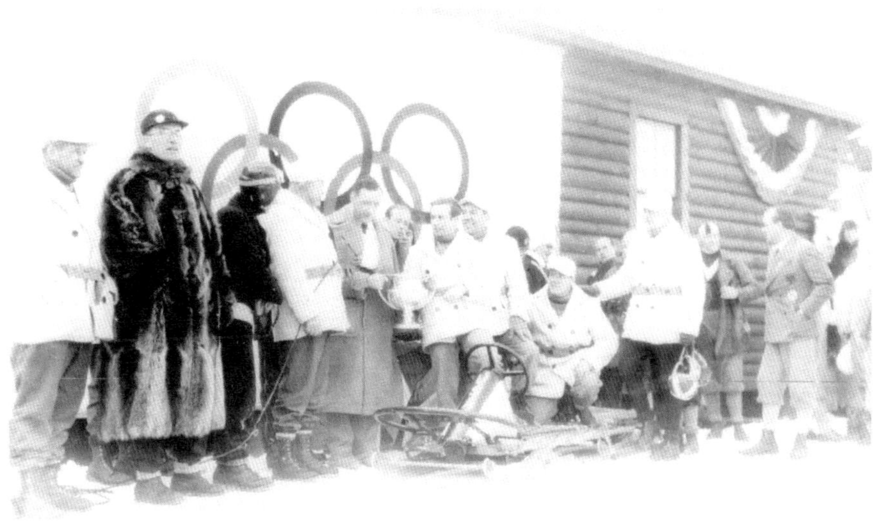

Presentation of the Martineau Challenge Cup to the USA I Four-Man Bobsled Team after their win at the 1932 Winter Olympics. Godfrey Dewey is in the fur coat, second from left. *Collection of the 1932 & 1980 Lake Placid Winter Olympic Museum.*

of Lake Placid, winter in the snow belt of this country is permitted to play its beneficent part in building stronger minds in stronger bodies for all who embrace what it so lavishly offers."

By 1927, Lake Placid had created such a reputation that Godfrey Dewey was asked unofficially if the town would consider hosting the 1932 Olympic Winter Games. It was the intent of the Olympic Committee to hold the winter and summer games in the same country. Since Los Angeles had been awarded the summer games, the committee was looking for a U.S. resort to host the winter games. Could the little village of Lake Placid (population four thousand) host such a huge international event?

The first Winter Olympics had been held in Chamonix, France, in 1924, and the second was about to be held in St. Moritz, Switzerland. Godfrey Dewey traveled to Europe to study the winter sports and attend the 1928 games. He officially went to the Olympics as leader of the U.S. ski team but spent a lot of time studying the organization and operation of the games. Somehow, he even got the job of carrying the American flag at the opening ceremony. When he returned home, he was convinced that Lake Placid could host the games in a fashion that rivaled Europe.

Unfortunately, as Lake Placid was deciding if it wanted to be host, other towns had stepped forward to vie for the 1932 games. Bids came from Yosemite Valley and Lake Tahoe, California; Bear Mountain, New York; Duluth and Minneapolis, Minnesota; and Denver, Colorado. If all U.S. resorts were eliminated, Montreal and Oslo were waiting.

It was difficult for Dewey to persuade the committee to pick the little town of Lake Placid. The Californians desperately wanted both the summer and winter games in their state and were willing to spend huge amounts of money to make it happen. The Scandinavians refused to believe any American town could provide Olympic facilities.

By working hard, pulling strings and hedging bets, Dewey sold his bid to the Olympic Committee. "The award was made to Lake Placid because of its pre-eminent standing as a winter sports resort, its climate and terrain, its existing sports facilities, its experience in staging winter sports, and its guarantee that the additional facilities necessary for the conduct of the Games would be provided." For the first time in history, the Olympic Winter Games would be held in North America.

Two facilities missing at Lake Placid were a bobsled run and a Cresta run. As Dewey had hoped, Cresta was soon dropped as an Olympic event. Now, Lake Placid needed only a bobsled run, but it would have to be a good one—a match for the famous European runs. Since the village of Lake Placid did not have the money to build such an expensive facility, the state had promised to build it.

The building of the bobsled run "triggered one of the shortest but most significant battles in the controversy over Forever Wild," the provision in the New York State Constitution that outlawed man-made structures on publicly owned Forest Preserve lands. In 1929, the state legislature passed a bill authorizing funds to build, equip and maintain a bobsled run "on lands in which any necessary easement may be provided without cost to the state," most likely privately owned land. A few weeks later, the legislature passed a second bill, providing for the run to be built on state land.

It had been determined that the best site for the run was on state land on the western slope of the Sentinel Range due east of Lake Placid. Because the state constitution mandated that these be "forever kept as wild forest lands," state officials knew there might be trouble. They pushed the issue by starting to construct the run and waiting to see what happened. And things did happen! The Association for the Protection of the Adirondacks opposed the plan, contending that the run would require the illegal removal of at least twenty-five hundred trees and that the speed, danger and thrill of bobsledding were incompatible with land set aside under wilderness and watershed protection. The battle went to the courts.

The appellate division found the "Bobsled Bill" unconstitutional. The case was then argued before the court of appeals, and on March 18, 1930, the court agreed. A bobsled run could not be built on state land. Judge Frederick C. Crane wrote an opinion that firmly upheld the Forever Wild clause. Trees could not be cut to make room for bobsled courses, tennis courts, baseball parks or other recreational facilities.

Once state-owned sites were eliminated, attention turned to a proposed site on private land. A bobsled run was about to be built on Mount Jo, overlooking Heart Lake.

Godfrey Dewey now pulled a fast one. He announced that he found the Mount Jo site less than satisfactory and had been searching for an alternative. He proposed a new site, eight miles east of Lake Placid, known as South Mountain or South Meadow Mountain. Its summit rose 2,960 feet, and its north slope had the proper grade for a bobsled course. The Lake Placid Club owned the land and would give the state an easement to build the run.

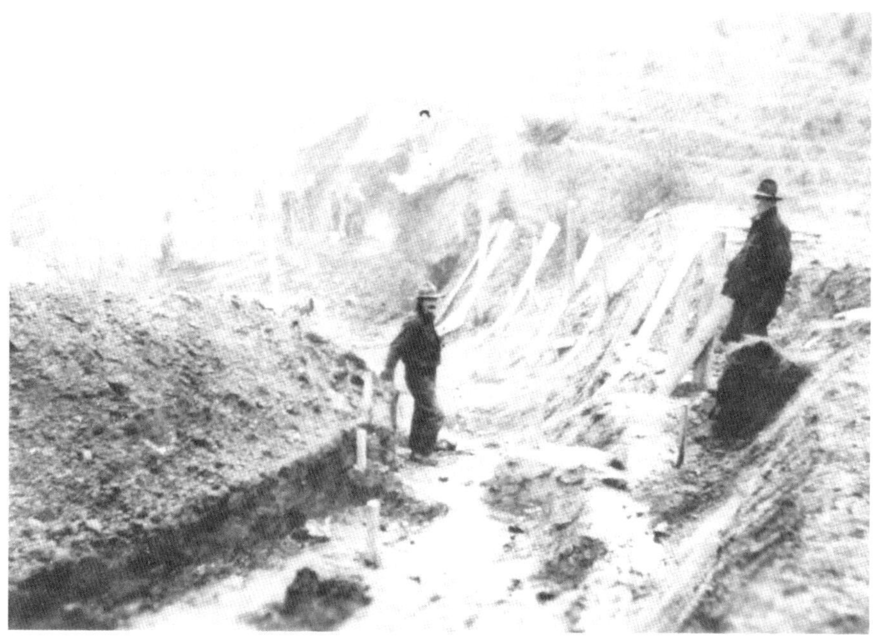

Construction of the Mount Van Hoevenberg bobsled run. *Collection of the 1932 & 1980 Lake Placid Winter Olympic Museum.*

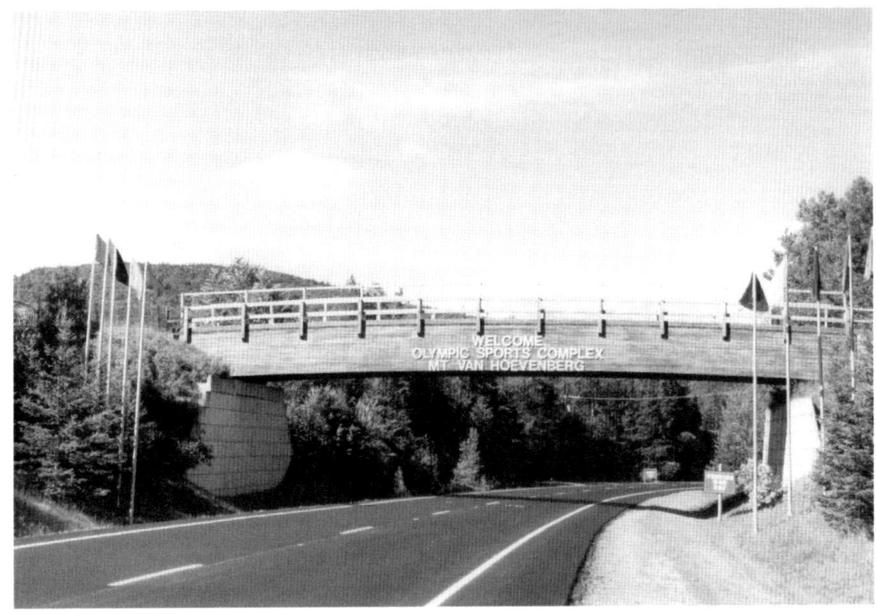

Entrance to the Mount Van Hoevenberg Winter Sports Complex.

The state agreed to the new site and to a change in the mountain's name to one of Olympic prominence. A suggestion to call it Roosevelt Mountain was rejected. Godfrey Dewey suggested Mount Van Hoevenberg in honor of the figure who once roamed the woods and mountains surrounding the site.

Mount Van Hoevenberg became the site of the first bobsled run not only in the United States but also in the entire Western Hemisphere. It was used for the 1932 and 1980 Winter Olympic Games, when a luge run was added, and for many other major competitions. A Nordic ski center was also added to make the site a complete winter recreation complex.

It seems fitting that Henry's name was placed on a winter playground. For although it was created many years after Henry Van Hoevenberg tramped through the area, he was one of the pioneers who made it happen. The III Olympic Winter Games Committee recognized this in its official report issued after the conclusion of the 1932 games:

> *The Games could never have been awarded to Lake Placid if it had not been for the international standing that this resort had attained as a winter-sports center. So the history of the Games in reality goes back to that day, over a quarter of a century ago, when organized enjoyment of the sports*

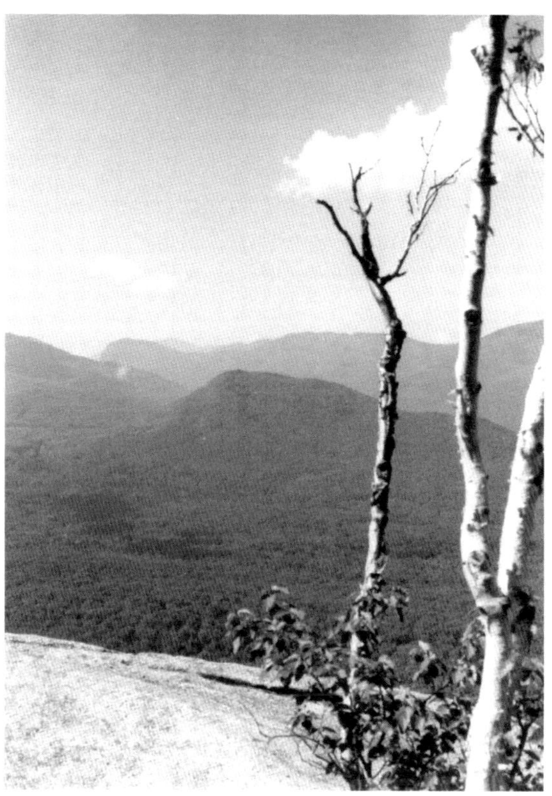

Mount Jo from Mount Van Hoevenberg.

> *of snow and ice and cold began where the highest peaks of the Adirondack mountains cast their shadows on the village by the two lakes.*

Surely, "Mr. Van" would be thrilled to see that the winter of 1904 set in motion a series of events that would result in Lake Placid becoming the premier winter resort of America. And Mr. Van would like his Mount Van Hoevenberg—one side groomed for zooming bobsleds, luges and cross-country skiers, and the other side growing wild and green, watchful of South Meadow and Mount Jo.

Fare-Thee-Well

My time is fast passing to view these grand mountains,
And the grand scenes of Nature that about them I see,
Of great boulder rocks and sweet crystal fountains,

Fresh from their Creator they have all come to me.
And I must soon leave to unborn generations,
Those scenes that so long have been dear to my sight,
Who will hereafter view them with varied emotions,
And volumes about them great Authors will write.
Oh! the old feldspar mountains, with their sweet crystal fountains,
The evergreen mountains we all love so well!
—Orson S. Phelps, "Mountain Song"

If I let my imagination run free, I can suppose that little has changed since "Old Mountain" Phelps viewed "the grand scenes of Nature" about Mount Marcy. When I stand on the summit, I still get that "heaven up-h'isted-ness" feeling. I still see the great boulders and the brilliant waterfalls. I see the feldspar and the acres upon acres of evergreens. And they seem fresh and vibrant and pristine.

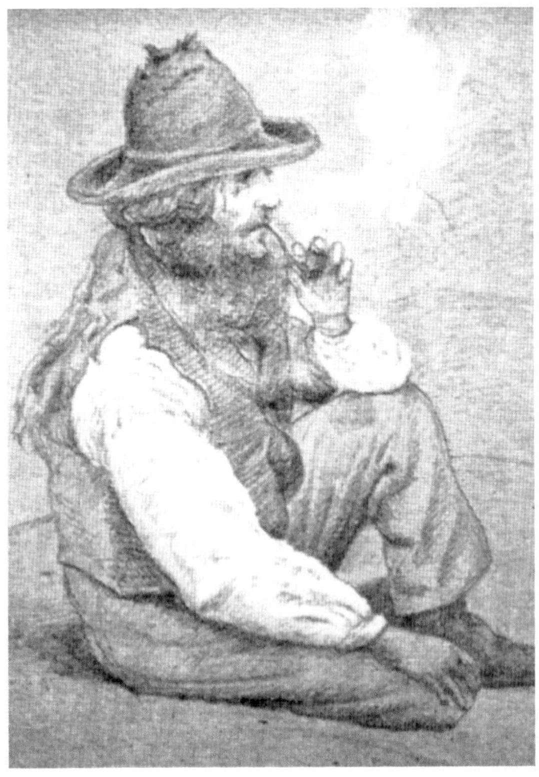

Orson "Old Mountain" Phelps guided many tourists up Mount Marcy in the 1800s. *From a pencil sketch by Frederick B. Allen.*

But the reality is that the scene has greatly changed; 90 percent of the forest is second growth, not old growth. Thousands upon thousands of human feet have stepped onto the anorthosite since Phelps's generation. Many simply admired the scene. But some trampled alpine flora. Some pitched tents. Some strapped on skis while others wore snowshoes. A few died. One became president of the United States.

Horses hauled stones and generators up the mountain. Huts and signal towers were built and later destroyed. Fires and axes assaulted the slopes. More recently, hikers hauled out garbage and hauled in grass seed and rocks to restore the summit vegetation. The improvements over the last twenty years are tremendous. Mount Marcy has undergone much change—change for the better. It is one of the few places on earth where "the grand scenes of Nature" have been restored.

But like Phelps, I wonder what the next generation will think of these scenes. Will they be able to feel the natural rhythms of the mountain?

In the summer of 2000, I took my daughter Marcy on her first trip up Mount Marcy. I wanted to show her the place that I love so well. Though she was only eight years old, she was eager to follow the footsteps of Old Mountain Phelps along Johns Brook to Slant Rock and beyond. When we reached the timberline, Marcy turned into a mountain goat and climbed on all fours over the wrinkled rocks.

I led her to the bronze plaque, and she read the words out loud. Then we climbed to the top of the rock slab and stood on the highest point of the mountain. Marcy spread her arms and leaned into the wind.

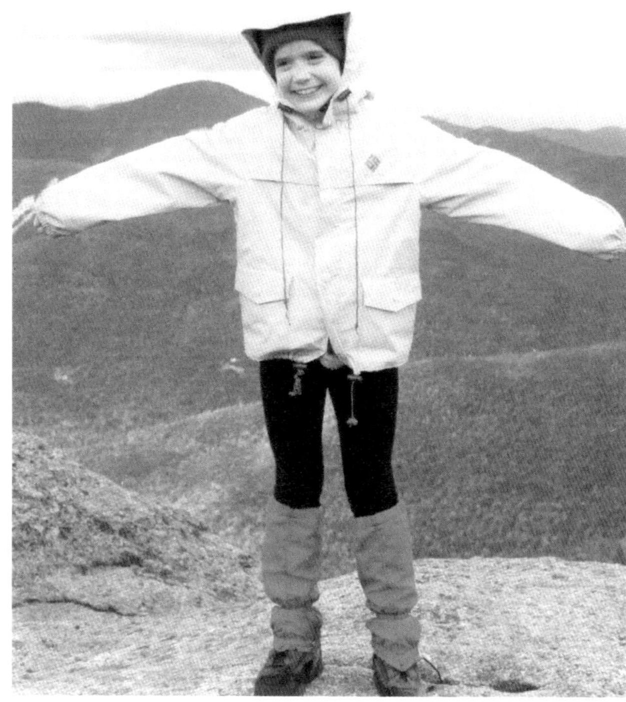

Marcy Weber, age eight, on Mount Marcy in 2000. *Photo by William L. Weber III.*

Mount Marcy

The wind lifts my soul.
My soul lifts my spirit and makes me rise, too.
I fly with the falcon.
I zoom through the water with the otter and beaver.
I fly again.
I fly over many mountains.
I land and zoom back down on the wings I have.
Down to the valley.
—Marcy Weber, 2000

Mount Marcy is a space where even the youngest of souls can feel the elements and connect with natural forces. They can see the wildlife, rivers, forests and fragile alpine ecosystem that once dominated the whole countryside. They can enjoy a sense of timeless landscape. This is a rare experience in today's world.

The "old feldspar mountain" that we call Mount Marcy is invaluable and irreplaceable terrain. There is no mountain in the world quite like it. We must safeguard it. We must preserve it for unborn generations. So the wind can lift their soul. So they can spread wings and split clouds.

Adirondack Women

Writing Gone Astray

People often ask, "What made you want to be an author?" I usually give the appropriate answer: "I enjoy writing." I guess I am afraid to reveal the true answer: "cloth diapers."

After the birth of my second daughter, I spent hours at the clothesline hanging and folding diapers and dreaming about the Adirondack Mountains. Before we had children, my husband and I spent every free weekend hiking, canoeing, skiing and snowshoeing in the beautiful wilderness up north. I hoped that someday we could share our Adirondack adventures with Emily and Marcy.

At ages one and two, the girls were too young for hiking or skiing, but I thought that it was time to introduce them to the mountains in some way. I had plenty of time for thinking and an occasional free hand. What if I wrote children's stories about the Adirondacks? I could teach them about the mountains and nature and animals. I could tell stories about girls who were strong and free and courageous.

I soon discovered a folktale about a farm girl named Esther and knew that I had found my story. In 1839, the young farm girl Esther McComb dreamed about climbing to the top of Whiteface Mountain. Reminders that "girls should be spinning and baking" and that "the woods are full of danger" did not sway her. Esther set off to climb Whiteface, became lost and spent a stormy night in the woods but discovered a new mountain and new happiness. The mountain was named Esther Mountain and is still the only Adirondack high peak named for a woman.

At a writing workshop, I scribbled my first draft of the story and was encouraged by the instructor to pursue the book. However, she suggested that I check some of the historical details.

The next month, I traveled to the Adirondack Museum and began what I thought would be a few hours of historical research. The research lasted two years and took me, my husband and my daughters to libraries, museums, cemeteries and courthouses. The four of us traveled throughout upstate New York discovering bits and pieces of information about Esther. We walked the wooded trails around Esther Mountain and explored stone bridges, quarries, kilns and cellar holes.

Finally, I completed my middle-grade historical fiction and sent out several query letters. All the publishers responded with rejections. No one wanted my Esther story.

I felt that someone must be interested; I had uncovered some fascinating details about Esther's life. I had collected stacks of information about the mountain—its formation, settlers, logging history and stewards. Was there another market beyond the children's market? Would adults be interested in an account of the mountain?

I queried a regional publisher and proposed a natural and social history book for adults. Within weeks, I had a $100 advance and a signed contract.

Before the book was completed, I collaborated with folksinger Peggy (Eyres) Lynn to write the song "Esther," which was later recorded on CD. Although the song is about Esther's struggle up the mountain, the last verse is my mantra about writing:

If you dare to set out on a mountain,
And find you've somehow gone astray,
Though you miss your final destination,
Look at what you've learned along the way.

I never intended to write a history book, but there it was. And a folksong, too. And more. An artist created an etching of Esther for the book cover. A women's group designed and sold Esther T-shirts. A group of sixty people climbed to the summit of Esther Mountain for a celebration of poetry, song and inspiration.

I still keep working on the Esther children's story, and it keeps being rejected. Maybe someday it will be printed. The story deserves it. It has given me so much. It made me take a step. It made me climb a mountain. It made me an author.

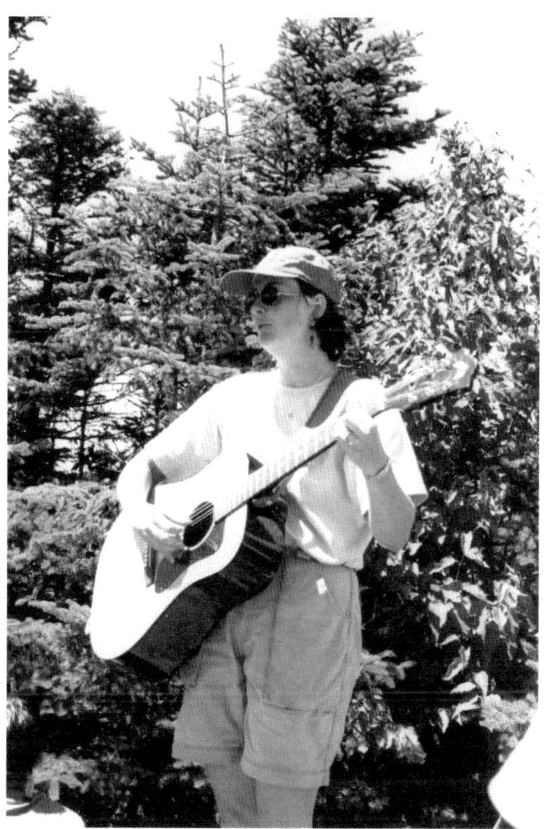

Folksinger/songwriter Peggy Lynn performing "Esther" at a celebration on Esther Mountain on July 30, 1995.

Sometimes I lament that I have not reached my destination. I did not give my daughters their Esther book. Then, I realize that I gave them something more meaningful. I reached my true destination. I shared the Adirondacks with them. Together, we discovered fir waves and log troughs and stagecoaches. We learned about Esther and about one another.

I hope my writing projects keep going astray.

Girl Gone Wild

Pioneering Journalist Kate Field Made the Adirondacks Her Beat

Like masses of vacationers, Kate Field set out on her first visit to the Adirondacks in the summer of 1869. Reverend William H.H. Murray's 236-page book, *Adventures in the Wilderness, or Camp-Life in the Adirondacks*, lured her and many others. The travel guide mixed how-to advice with a collection of fanciful backwoods stories and caused phenomenal excitement. It supposedly "kindled a thousand campfires and taught a thousand pens how to write of nature," according to orator Wendell Phillips.

Most of these writers were hunters and fishermen, but one outsider in the throngs was Field (1838–1896). Here was no ordinary spinster; born Mary Katherine Keemle Field, the daughter of an actor father and a Philadelphia Quaker mother, she left her home in St. Louis at age sixteen and went to Boston to live with her millionaire aunt and uncle, Mr. and Mrs. Milton H. Sanford. They supported her lavishly and even took her to Paris, Rome and Florence, where she came to know the social and cultural elite. She became an unorthodox crusader of many social causes and one of the first female reporters, writing for the *New York Tribune*, the *New York Herald*, the *Atlantic Almanac* and other papers. Later, she launched *Kate Field's Washington*.

It wasn't so peculiar that Field went to the Adirondacks—plenty of fashionable women attired themselves in muslin and silk and promenaded on a porch at some grand hotel—but Field took Murray's advice and camped out in the woods. "To come into the Wilderness and not camp out would be to me as unnatural as to bathe in a diver's water-proof suit," wrote Field in the *New York Tribune*.

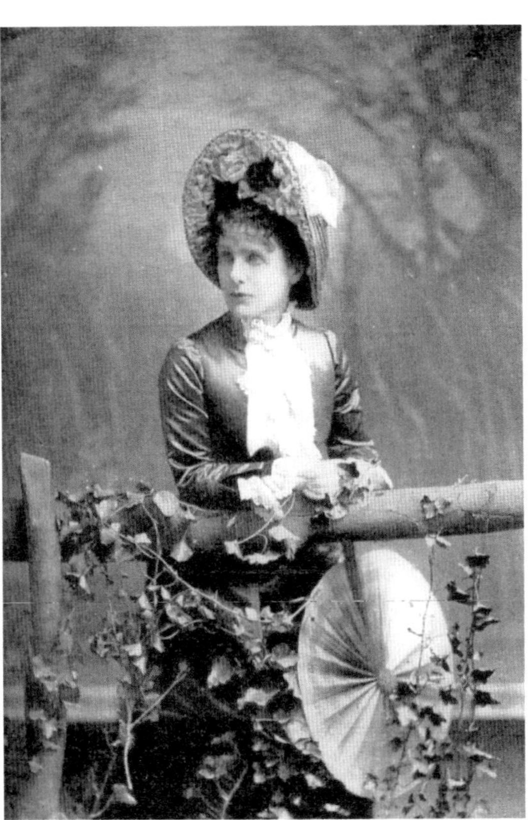

Kate Field, 1865.

Field's views were decidedly unconventional. In 1870, in the *Atlantic Almanac*, she wrote that her critics had called her and some female hiking companions "maniacs." The admonitions did not deter Field, but in case things turned out poorly, she explained somewhat sarcastically, "I made my will. I had nothing, and left it, without reservation, to my relations."

Field plunged into the woods, traveling from Plattsburgh to Lower Saranac Lake to Raquette Lake. She fished, hunted, searched for birch bark to make into dainty boxes, climbed mountains, sang merry songs and sat by the fire at night. But little danger met her there.

Her writings are filled with humor and an appreciation of local wit rarely found in early Adirondack literature. She noted a native man's opinion about prohibition laws: "We're a law unto ourselves. When there's no laws, there's no transgressors." In general, she observed that true Adirondackers endure rain, mud and black flies and yet cheerfully declare, "Whatever is, is right."

As for the complaints of local sportsmen that their favorite hunting and fishing grounds had been overrun by tourists, Field put forth a populist viewpoint: "The greatest good of the greatest number is, I believe, the true democratic platform, and if several hundred men think that the life-giving principles of the North Woods was [*sic*] instituted for the benefit of a few guns and rods, they are sadly mistaken."

Not surprisingly, her remarks brought sharp reprisal. Sportsman and writer Thomas Bangs Thorpe was upset that the Adirondacks had been invaded by Miss Kate Field. He thought that ladies had nothing in their education that made them appreciate such places.

This was drivel, felt Field. She had developed a great affection for the region, and she expressed concerns about misuses of the woods. Thorpe advocated clearing an eighteen- to twenty-foot square of woods to erect a shanty, while Field advised her readers to bring a tent rather than kill trees. "It is cruel to stab a tree to the heart merely to secure a small strip of bark," she said. "It is ungrateful to destroy the pine and balsam that have given us our beds of boughs, and fanned us with their vital breath. Let there be tents."

Clearly, this writer valued the region's magnificence and was adding a woman's voice to the idea of preserving the wilderness. In the *New York Times*, Samuel H. Hammond had suggested marking out "a circle of a hundred miles in diameter" and making it a "forest forever," while surveyor Verplanck Colvin recommended an "Adirondack Park or timber preserve" be created to ensure a future water supply. Field believed in preserving the region not only for its waters and forests but also for its recreational values. She wrote that the Adirondack Mountains "were intended by Nature to be the Eastern pleasure-ground of the United States."

Field authored four books that garnered good reviews, including one on Dickens. On March 3, 1869, she debuted as a lecturer, presenting "Women in the Lyceum" and was well received in this endeavor, too. No doubt her cultivated voice and dazzling appearance had something to do with her effectiveness as a speaker. The tall figure, with soft curls in her long hair, was usually attired in a Paris gown and adorned with jewels. Abolitionist William Lloyd Garrison commented that it was worth an admission fee just to see Kate Field on the platform, as she made so lovely a picture.

For her second lecture, Field chose the Adirondacks as her subject. Once again, she met with high praise; even a refined audience in Chicago found her delightful and charming. On February 8, 1870, the *Chicago Tribune* ran a long review about Field's "Among the Adirondacks" lecture, calling it "An Unqualified Success."

The *Tribune* described how she held up the mirror of nature, and the audience was enraptured. "Following her scampering feet," the paper reported, "the but too willing audience passed over green fields, crossed babbling brooks, or rapid torrents, ascended mountains, descended into verdure-clad and smiling valleys, viewed cataracts…slept under the dome of the midnight sky, and did a hundred other things they never dreamed of doing before."

It was not possible for the reviewer to give an outline of the lecture "without marring its literary and artistic beauty," so he repeated only a few gems, such as the advice Field and her companions had been given as women attempting a woods excursion. Field said, "There were four of us, and all women. 'Four women!' exclaimed our critics. 'Order four coffins, and take them with you.'"

"We took the dilemma (not the coffins) at once by the horns," she continued,

> *and constituted ourselves the Black Fly Club, for there is nothing like calling things by their right names. And now that I live to tell the moving tale, let me say to women, that they can go anywhere, and do anything, provided they conduct themselves properly. Of course, it would be absurd that it is not much more agreeable to be accompanied by the tyrant called "man;" but, when there are no tyrants to come to lovely woman's rescue, it is astonishing how well lovely woman can rescue herself, provided she exerts the brain and muscle given her by the Creator thousands of years ago, and not entirely annihilated by long disuse.*

Field recalled the awesome scene of tall mountains with black frowns on their brows. "This is the place for echoes," the guide had told Field's party.

"And we broke the stillness with a trill that excited much indignation from owls and ravens," said Field. "The mountains have good ears. They no sooner caught the strain than with glorious breadth of lungs they repeated note for note. One, two, three, four, five, six, seven, eight, nine, ten, eleven, twelve reverberations. We laughed, and the hills were in one round of merriment."

Field then described a deer hunt. It was a chilly night, so she wrapped herself in blankets as she sat in the center of the boat. As they meandered along the creek, not a word was spoken. "The paddler dips his blade as if it were of phantom stuff," said Field, "and the hunter, who likewise acts as pilot, indicates by the raising of his arms, in what direction the boat shall be steered." Hours passed until "out of the darkness peer two balls of fire—the deer's eyes."

A shot is fired, and soon "a noble buck is found, stark and stiff, dead among the lilies to which he went for life." As the hunting party heads back to camp, "northern lights shoot up…like a choir of white-robed angels, with wide-spread wings, that you almost hear them sing," recalled Field. "Far off flickers your campfire, which serves as a beacon."

Field's mesmerizing recollection of the hunt caused the *Tribune* reviewer to remark: "After such a description, who would not go deer hunting (with dears)?"

The lecture was concluded with a beautiful tribute to the memory of John Brown. Field said that she could not leave the Adirondacks without making a pilgrimage to his North Elba grave. Standing beside John Brown's tomb, "plucking roses and buttercups that sprang from the giant's heart," she envisioned the entire history of America's Civil War.

"Skilled in mountain strategy, I saw John Brown come to the Adirondacks, in 1849," she said, "hoping to find the nucleus of a black army in the colony of fugitive slaves to whom Gerrit Smith had given lands in Essex County. I saw him turn to the stouter, sterner mind and muscle of his own sons, reared to look God and nature in the face, he still clinging to the Adirondacks, as if from them came inspiration."

Field then recounted scenes of Brown fighting at Harpers Ferry, lying wounded in jail and hanging dead. She talked of the dark and stormy night that followed the execution, precursor of the war to come. Then, just two years after the execution, she saw Union soldiers marching into battle, singing "John Brown's Body." It seemed to her that John Brown's lessons would endure forever. "The moral of the Adirondacks is freedom!" she concluded. "Off with your hats, down on your knees, fire minute guns over the grave, sing the hymn that gave us liberty, for 'John Brown's Soul is marching on.'"

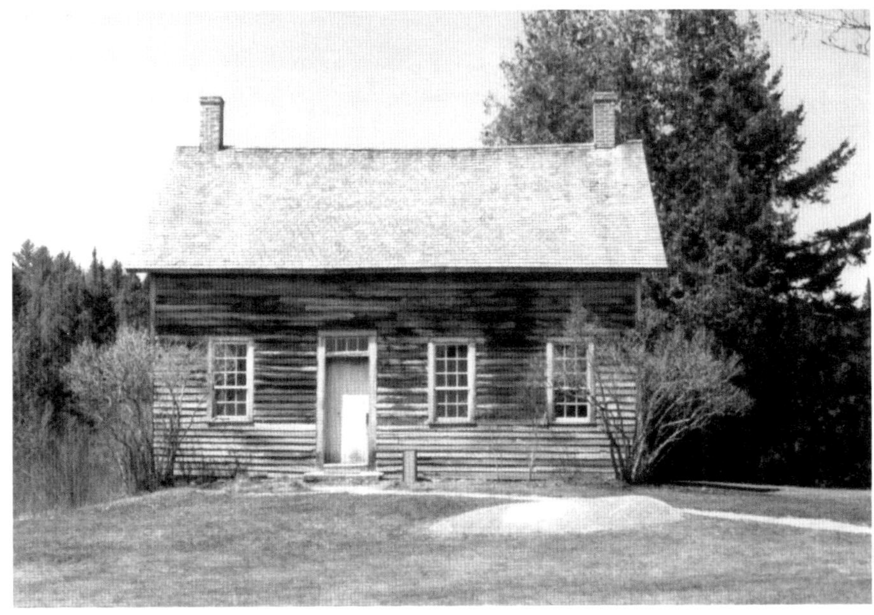

John Brown's farmhouse in North Elba, New York.

Just a few months before her Chicago lecture, Field helped ensure that John Brown's legacy would endure. She contributed $100, and convinced nineteen others to do the same, toward the purchase of John Brown's farm and grave site in North Elba. In 1896, the group transferred ownership to New York State.

This was a lasting gift, and David Baldwin, in *Notable American Women, 1607–1950*, found Kate Field "more than a tedious dilettante." He said she displayed humor, courage and dramatic flair, and her life "shows the degree of independence a clever and intelligent American woman of her time could attain."

Field faced society's glare and held to her unconventional ways. She never married, she had a career and earned her own money and she was an activist in issues such as international copyright, Hawaiian annexation, temperance, Mormon polygamy and women's suffrage. But her legacy faded. She is largely remembered only for one of her sayings: "They talk about a woman's sphere, as though it had a limit. There's not a place in earth or heaven. There's not a task to mankind given…without a woman in it." In the nascent field of Adirondack preservation, Kate Field was the woman in it.

Martha Reben, Wilderness Health Seeker

In 1998, Franklin County chose to honor Martha Reben as a distinguished woman in history. A sign along River Street in Saranac Lake reads:

Wilderness Lady
Martha Reben
1911–1964.
Her life here and her books about the Adirondacks inspired many.

Martha Reben is the pen name of Martha Ruth Rebentisch, born in Manhattan on April 30, 1906. (She later misrepresented her age, leading to the conclusion that she was born in 1911.) Her mother died of tuberculosis when Martha was six years old, and Martha became afflicted with the disease at age sixteen. She was terribly sick when she left New York City and came to the Adirondacks in 1927.

Saranac Lake was the famed haven for tuberculosis patients, so Martha's father sent her there, to Trudeau's sanitarium. Dr. Trudeau's original treatment included fresh air, rest and exercise and entertainment. But soon it had developed into months of bed rest, a passive existence and operations. This was the regimen given to Martha.

After three years of bed rest, she did not seem any better. Therapies such as gas, tuberculin, shot bags and two nerve operations did not help either. Actually, the nerve operation caused her paralyzed left lung to shrink, leaving her with only one working lung. The doctors wanted to do a third operation. Martha decided that surgery would probably kill her, so she was willing to try just about any other kind of treatment.

By chance, she saw an advertisement in the local paper: "Wanted: To get in touch with some invalid who is not improving, and who would like to go into the woods for the summer."

The ad had been placed by Fred Rice, a local woodsman and boat builder who believed the outdoors was the best treatment for invalids. He had watched tuberculosis patients heal from peace and quiet in the woods. He thought it would be a good way to help someone and for him to make a few dollars.

What was the response to the ad? "The only invalid who had the courage to act against the influence of her environment was a young woman," he said. The fifty-five-year-old man hadn't expected a young woman as his patient. Nor had he expected someone so very sick who was city bred and had never been in the woods. But that is what he got in Martha.

Fred needed the money, so he didn't refuse Martha, but he thought her chances of being cured were not favorable. He recalled, "I told her that I believed she might make a partial recovery at once by going into the forest and living under the conditions I have described, and that it was possible she might be cured."

Of course, Martha's doctors protested her plan to take the outdoor treatment. Her friends and family were "shocked and incredulous," but Martha did not let that stop her. She had no idea what was going to happen in the woods, but it had to be better than life in the hospital.

In June 1931, Fred took Martha in his boat *Gull* through Lower Saranac Lake and Middle Saranac Lake to Weller Pond. She was too weak to sit up during the twelve-mile trip, so she had to ride on a mattress propped across the seats of the boat.

Finally, they arrived at the campsite. "The noonday sun was beating down onto the dry, piny campsite and the air was fragrant with pitch when I stepped ashore," wrote Martha. "I had no clear idea of what a real woodsman's camp looked like, but certainly I had not expected anything like this." What she saw was a drooping tent, a single bed supported on the ground by rocks, blackened pots and pans, a moldy green table and the noticeable lack of chairs, or even boxes, to sit on. There was also no stove, no faucet and no toilet.

Fred cooked meals over a campfire, told stories and sometimes took her for boat rides. "[D]uring the first week everything was new to her," recalled Fred, "and therefore it was the most interesting week of her life…she gave little thought to illness."

Martha had started a new life, a life of camping and observing wildlife. She enjoyed listening to the hoot of the owl, the drumming of the partridge, the call of the loon and the voices of the gulls, hawks, ducks, eagles and herons. By the end of the week, she was strong enough to walk around camp and to go fishing for perch and pike.

After her time at the pond, Martha did not want to go back to the hospital, so she went to live at Fred's house in Saranac Lake. She slept on her hospital bed in the boat shop, which was heated with an old box stove. She quickly became friends with Fred's wife, Kate, and grandson, John Benson.

The return to town shocked Martha. She wrote:

> *What I saw now filled me with dismay. As I rode through the heart of the village in a taxi, the streets looked narrow and crowded, the fronts of the houses and stores indescribably dingy and ugly. I had forgotten how unlovely civilization really was.*

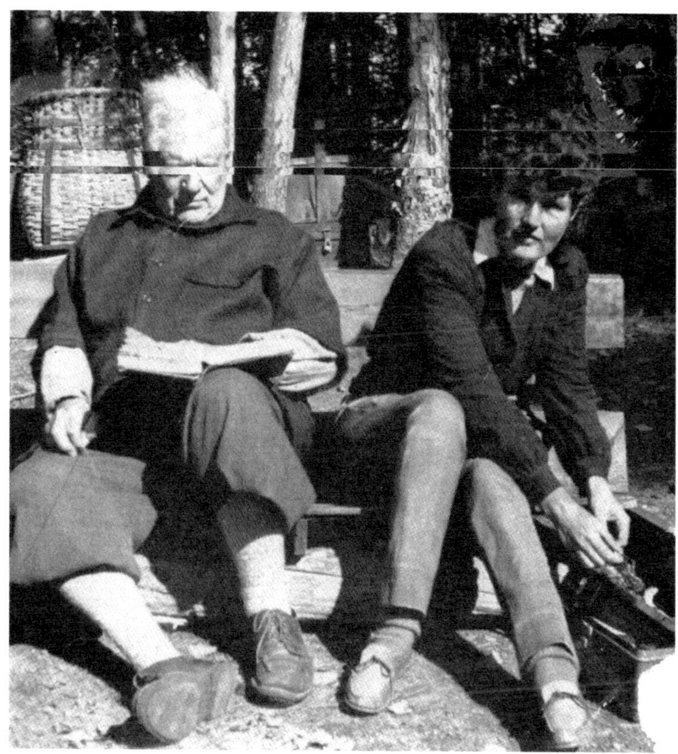

Fred Rice and Martha Reben. *Courtesy of the Adirondack Collection, Saranac Lake Free Library.*

> *Even the people looked strange now, especially the women with their gaudily painted lips and fingernails. After becoming accustomed to Mr. Rice's heavily tanned face (and my own in the mirror) I found every one else appeared woefully pale.*
>
> *In camp we looked out over the open lake and beyond to the hills and to the sky above and there was everywhere a feeling of freedom and of clean open space. If my eyes did not always see beauty there, they saw at least perfect harmony of line and color…I kept wishing that everybody could go into some form of isolation for a while, so that he could return with eyes undimmed by habit to see just what modern life offered him.*

Martha's spirit had improved; she had discovered a new way of looking at life. Her health had improved, too. When she visited her doctor, he was astonished by her good appearance. She went back to camp in 1932, and by the end of the summer, Fred thought, "insofar as I could see, she was well." Within a few years, she claimed that she was free of tuberculosis. In 1945, doctors examined her and found no indications of active TB.

When Martha met patients undergoing traditional treatments, they often warned her against exercise and sunlight. She sometimes responded that for her treatments, she was going to the greatest doctor of all—Nature.

Martha's friend, Mrs. D. Mott Chapin, who also had TB and was in recovery, did not really believe in the outdoor cure, but she came to visit Martha at Weller Pond in 1933. She found the campsite quite pleasing. "Fred and Martha had picked a point on the north shore of Weller Pond which was swept by any breeze that came across and which was high, dry and beautiful," she wrote. "Many large pines stood there but there was just enough open space so the morning sun could get in early…There is no doubt that this was the very best place for a camp on the whole lake and you could expect Fred and his knowledge of the woods to pick it."

Chapin kept extending her "short" visit until she had stayed the whole summer of 1933. She found Martha to have a quiet and serene personality and a delightful sense of humor. "There was a lot of joking going on around camp and she shared it with joy," Chapin recalled. "She seemed to be interested in many things and read all kinds of books…she was starting to write and she did a lot of it propped up in bed on pillows or under a tree somewhere."

Chapin described Fred as a heavy man, about five feet, ten inches tall and weighing at least two hundred pounds, with white hair and a jolly disposition. "We were always bothered by yellow-jackets who came to share with us and Fred ate with a fork in one hand and a fly swatter in the other." A mother raccoon and her babies would come, too. "The babies might climb up my pant leg and sit in my lap or try to swipe things off my plate…I remember they didn't shoo very well and Fred would swat them with the fly swatter."

Martha's interactions with the animals differed from Fred's. She found human characteristics in them and thought of them as friends. The keen observations she made in her books are often quite funny.

One of her friends was Mr. Dooley, a big, white Peking duck. Fred brought Dooley from the village in a pack basket and gave him to Martha as a gift. Dooley had a distinct personality. He strutted around camp and stuck out his chest proudly. However, he ran to Martha for protection from chipmunks and snakes. Strangest of all, this duck was afraid of water. Martha said he would go swimming only if she stood over him "like a lifeguard." She explained his routine for entering the water: "First, he would stand in shallow water, about up to his ankles, like a woman wading and afraid to get her skirts wet. Next he would test the temperature of the water with his bill, and, critically, drink a little. Then he would blow through his nostrils, to clean them, until he had churned the water into bubbles...Once afloat, Mr. Dooley became very mettlesome. He tossed water over his back, beat the water with his wings, and stood on his head with his tail pointing upward, to retrieve things from the bottom."

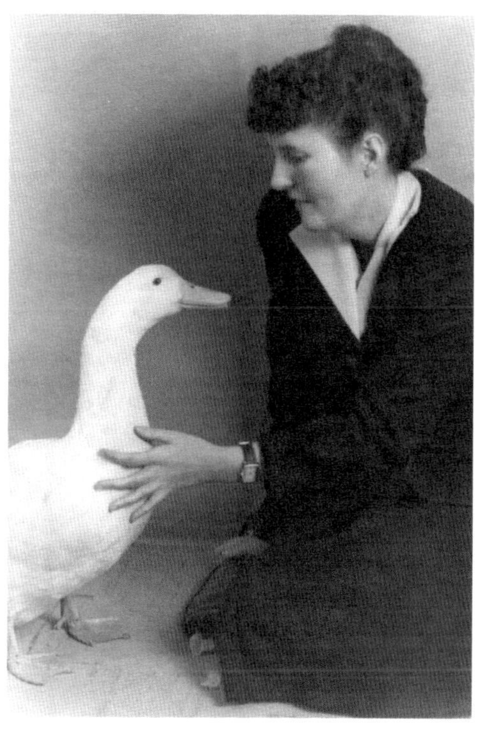

Martha Reben with Mr. Dooley. *Courtesy of the Adirondack Collection, Saranac Lake Free Library.*

Another animal friend was a small skunk that Martha got from Florida. He seemed to like to bite fingers, so Fred put the skunk in a barrel and told Martha to stay away from it until he could make a harness for the skunk. But Martha could not resist. She reached into the barrel. The skunk hung onto her finger so tightly that Fred had to choke the animal to get it away from Martha's finger. When Fred asked her why she put her hand in the barrel, she said that she wanted to pacify the skunk. "I guess the little pet was not a pacifist!" remarked Fred.

Martha adopted another pet, a raccoon, and named him Rufus. Fred was not particularly fond of the animal since he often pestered the old man. Rufus liked to sleep, covered in mud, on Fred's best flannel shirt. The coon chewed Fred's glasses case and his shoes, and sometimes he tied knots in Fred's shoelaces. One day, he stole Fred's false teeth.

Rufus did not reserve his mischief for Fred only. He had his own special ways of harassing Martha, too:

> *Sometimes I fastened my hair back in a pony tail, and there were few things he liked better than to slip up behind me and get hold of it. He would give it a good yank, then hang on determinedly (coons are surprisingly strong for their size), digging his toes in to brace himself while we carried on a tug of war, with me yelling and wildly feeling around behind me to get hold of him, while he managed to stay just out of my reach. I think the nearest we*

came to parting, though, was the time he found a rotting fish and carried it up onto my bed to eat it.

Martha developed a special bond with animals and with nature. Years later, she recalled one special moment:

I sat alone before my campfire one evening, watching as the sunset colors deepened to purple, the sky slowly darkened, and the stars came out. A deep peace lay over the woods and waters…

The moon came up behind the black trees to the east, and the wilderness stood forth, vast, mysterious, still. All at once the silence and the solitude were touched by wild music, thin as air, the faraway gabbling of geese flying at night.

Presently I caught sight of them as they streamed across the face of the moon, the high, excited clamor of their voices tingling through the night, and suddenly I saw, in one of those rare moments of insight, what it means to be wild and free. As they went over me, I was there with them, passing over the moonlit countryside, glorying with them in their strong-hearted journeying, exulting in its joy and splendor.

From 1931 to 1941, Martha spent summers at Weller Pond, enjoying the wildlife, improving her health and writing. Years later, she collected her writings into a 250-page manuscript, which she revised four times before she thought it was good enough for publication. It was published in 1952 as *The Healing Woods*, with the subtitle: "How my search for health in the woods opened up a new way of life." It was a bestseller and was featured by the Family Book Club.

Like fellow recluse and nature lover Henry David Thoreau, Martha Reben wrote a romantic version of her adventures. In *The Healing Woods*, she made herself younger and compressed time, squeezing several summers into one to make her recovery more dramatic. She was probably much sicker and much more troubled than she claimed in the book. And she never mentioned her relationship with "Bill," to whom she dedicated the book. He was a TB patient whom she had known—and had a romance with—for five years before he died of the disease.

Later, Martha wrote *The Way of the Wilderness*, which described her life after leaving the pond and moving into the town of Saranac Lake. Since Martha was in better health, her father decided to bring her home to the city. He arrived at Fred's house and found Martha living in the boat shop. "As he stared at the unfinished walls and raftered ceiling, at the full water pails and tin dipper beside the enameled washbasin on its rough wooden shelf," wrote Martha, "I saw his deep respect for progress and property being subtly outraged."

When her father, Ernest Rebentisch, announced his intentions to take Martha, Fred said that he shouldn't hurry to do that. The father replied that he thought she was well enough. To this, Fred retorted, "I'd like to see her stay that way."

"Well, she'll have to go back some day, won't she?" asked Ernest. Martha knew it would be hard to make him understand that she could never go back to New York City.

And she never did. Martha had the courage to stand up to her family, to live simply and poorly, to face death and to embrace wilderness.

Martha had not been a writer before coming to the Adirondacks. But she needed to earn an income, so she attended journalism classes and started a new career. Shortly after Martha started her writing, she feared that she would have to give it up because typing put a strain on her heart. Fred declared that he would do her typing—a daunting task since he had never touched a typewriter. But he learned to use his two fingers to "hunt and peck" on the typewriter keys.

After Martha's first two books were published (in 1952 and 1955), Martha and Fred had more money. By then, Fred's physical health was failing. They could no longer go so far to camp, so Martha had a tent platform built on Lower Saranac. She also bought an aluminum boat with a thirty-five-horsepower motor, which was more stable and easier to operate than the 219-pound *Gull*.

In the spring of 1956, a great surprise arrived at Martha's doorstep. It was Cornelius Vanderbilt Whitney, a famous financier, industrialist and socialite. He had recently taken to making films and wanted to make a movie based on *The Healing Woods*. He was interested in depicting the Adirondacks because he was heir to Whitney Park, one of the largest private preserves in the region.

Martha signed a contract and was given an advance payment. So that Martha and Fred could help with the movie, they spent the summer at one of Whitney's camps on Fat Fish Pond. They went again for the summer of 1957. Then things fell apart. Whitney fell in love with the actress playing Martha. He divorced his wife and went out of the movie business. Martha's movie was never finished.

However, Martha did come away with some money. She used it to buy a three-room cabin on the bank of the Saranac River near Bloomingdale.

Martha kept writing, and her third book, *A Sharing of Joy*, was published in 1963. She died shortly afterward, on January 7, 1964. Though the official cause of death is unknown, it is supposed that she died of congestive heart failure, probably caused by the loss of her lung in the nerve operation.

Fred was very saddened by Martha's death. A few months after her passing, he wrote to his grandson, "Three different times I have been sitting at the table and asked Martha some thing and when she didn't answer, I looked around to see why she didn't—and remembered that she was never going to answer me again!...I wish that I had died and been buried with her!"

Martha's ashes were scattered at Weller Pond, as were Fred's when he died in 1966. A wooden slab is nailed to a tree at their campsite. It reads, "Reben Point. May this spot be kept as a memorial to Martha Reben, whose life, and books on her life here, have inspired so many."

Martha went to Weller Pond seeking health, but she found so much more. The ending paragraph of *The Healing Woods* states:

> *The wilderness did more than heal my lungs, however. While it dwarfed me by its immensity and made me conscious of my insignificance, yet it made me aware of the importance of being an individual, capable of thinking and feeling not what was expected of me, but only what my own reasoning told me was true. It taught me fortitude and self-reliance, and with its tranquility it bestowed upon me something which would sustain me as long as I lived: a sense of the freshness and the wonder which life in natural surroundings daily brings and a joy in the freedom and beauty and peace that exist in a world apart from human beings.*

THE LADIES AND THE TRAMP

Tramping up the rock steps of the corkscrew above Indian Falls, on the Van Hoevenberg trail to Mount Marcy, I feel myself slip into the shadows of the earliest women to make this steep climb in the 1850s and '60s. They were plucky pioneers hampered by fashion and even more so by society's attitudes about proper feminine behavior and by sportsmen who despised women in "their" woods.

Proper ladies did not go into the wilderness in the mid-1800s. They stayed at boardinghouses or camped at pretty lakes while the men hunted and climbed mountains. The prevailing notion was that women should show no athletic vigor or adventurous spirit. Perhaps it had more to do with long skirts, tight corsets, heels and layers of petticoats, which hampered easy movement.

Still, a handful of women were discovering the joys of hitching up their heavy floor-length skirts, getting muddy and embracing nature. Eliza, Harriet and Abigail Austin ascended Mount Washington, the highest peak in New Hampshire, in 1821, and by the 1840s, women ventured into the Catskill Mountains. In Maine in August 1849, two parties of women raced to be the first to reach the summit of Mount Katahdin.

Here in the Adirondacks in 1839, Esther Combs made an ascent of a peak beside Whiteface Mountain that now bears her name. Eleven years later, Anna Constable and her female friends trekked through the woods, camped in open lean-tos at Raquette Lake and climbed Blue Mountain. Hattie Wadhams climbed Whiteface in August 1859. And Mary Cook, Helen Lossing and Lucia Pychowska were among at least eleven women who climbed Mount Marcy before the end of the Civil War.

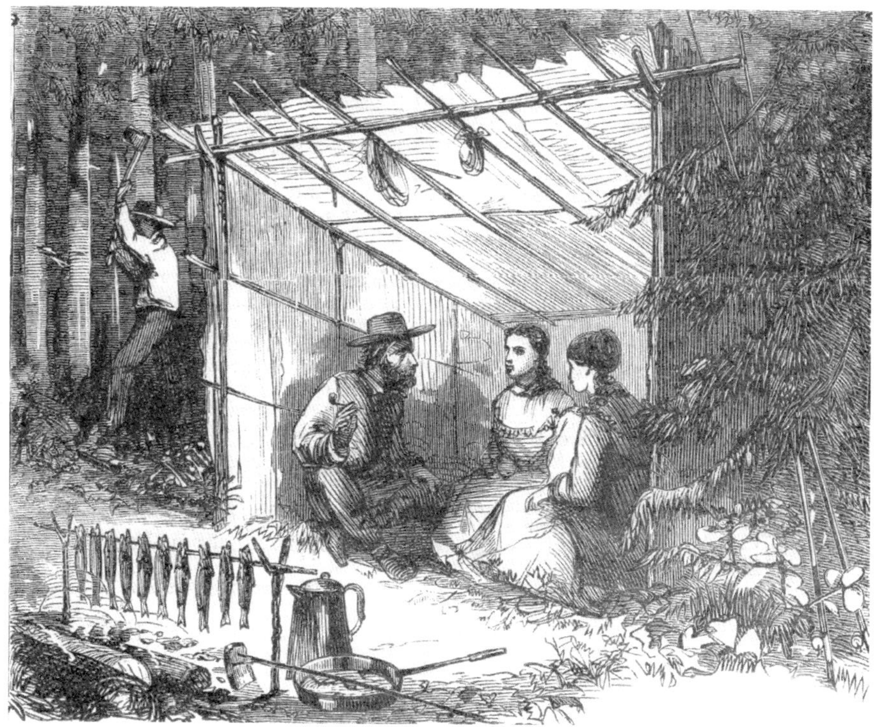

The Shanty, from the November 21, 1868 *Harper's Weekly*. *Drawn by Theodore R. Davis.*

Climbing Marcy was no tame walk in the woods back then. The mountain lay ten miles from the closest road, requiring at least two nights out. Guides were needed to lead the way through the pathless forest; carry gear, food and hunting rifles; fish, hunt and cook; build crude sleeping shanties; and protect the party from panthers, bears and wolves.

A century and a half later, my ascent of the mountain involves an eight-hour round-trip hike along a well-worn path. No camping required. I am my own guide. I don't need a rifle, there are no wolves and I carry my own gear and food. Of course, a proper Victorian lady would be wearing wool stockings, long skirts and a petticoat made of crinoline—a coarse stiff cotton fabric of horsehair and linen. A modern-day climb of the mountain requires only physical fitness, endurance and desire.

Understandably, few women ventured into the mountains in the 1800s. But by the mid-twentieth century, women were roaming the peaks, building and maintaining trails and helping lead local mountain clubs. In 1948, when the Adirondack Forty-Sixers elected their first officers, they chose Grace Hudowalski as president; Katherine Fletcher as secretary; and Orra Phelps as a director. And where once only men ventured, women now work as summit stewards and rangers and on trail crews.

But what about their nineteenth-century predecessors, those women who braved the ascending slopes and the condescending jeers and sneers? Their accomplishments were ridiculed and have been mostly forgotten—and they are not without some controversy.

In September 1859, *Harper's Monthly* printed T. Addison Richard's story of an ascent of Mount Marcy by a party consisting of four women. One sketch that accompanies the article is dated September 23, 1853, which would make it the first known climb of the mile-high pinnacle by a woman. (Historian Russell Carson disputed this, since Richards admitted that he wrote "to relieve the gravity of fact with the grace of fiction, as to present at the same time an instructive topography and an entertaining romance." But Richards's accompanying sketches show women shooting deer and reaching a summit.)

According to his story, Richards, a companion and two guides were walking along the road near McIntyre Iron Works when they met three ladies, their maid Marianna, three gentlemen, two guides and two hounds. The groups camped together and set out for the Lower Works—and Mount Marcy beyond—the next day.

The two-day journey proved difficult. One of Richards's sketches shows a lady clinging to a branch and gentlemen assisting two women as they clamber up a steep gully. The fourth woman stands atop a knoll triumphantly waving a flag.

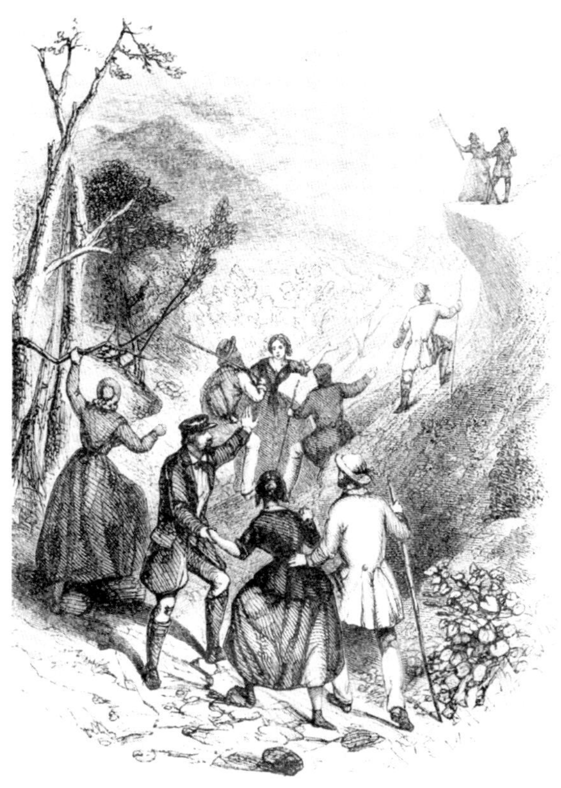

The ascent of Mount Marcy, circa 1853. *Drawn by T. Addison Richards.*

The entire group finally reached the summit, but we do not know how they regarded the view. We only know that Marianna "solemnly declared that she would not make the ascent again if the Queen of Sheba were coming up on the other side to meet her."

Five years later, Mary Cook, approaching from Keene Valley, conquered Marcy. "Long skirts and portly proportions notwithstanding," wrote one historian, "she climbed the highest of the Adirondacks and refused the aid of a rope around her waist to help her up the slide." Cook was heralded in September 1870 by the *Essex County Republican* as the first woman to stand on Marcy's summit, but two weeks later, the paper corrected itself, noting that Cook was the first who went "over the mountain and thro' the Indian Pass, and took what is called the 'Round Trip.'"

Cook, a painter, was accompanied by Miss Fannie Newton and artist Frederick S. Perkins. Their guide was the legendary Orson "Old Mountain" Phelps, who affectionately referred to the peak as "Mercy."

When they reached Marcy's summit, the group built a small hut from loose stones and covered it with moss. Inside, they left a paper that read: "This hospice, erected by a party from New York, August 19, 1858, is intended for the use and comfort of visitors to Tahawus.—F.S.P.—M.C.—F.M.N."

The next year, Helen Lossing of Poughkeepsie successfully ascended Marcy via the ironworks route. Her husband, Benson J. Lossing, documented and illustrated the climb in his book *The Hudson from the Wilderness to the Sea.*

Regarding the hiking attire of the fairer sex, Lossing wrote:

> *A woman needs a stout flannel dress, over shortened crinoline, of short dimensions, with loops and buttons to adjust its length; a hood and cape of the same materials, made so as to envelop the head and bust, and leave the arms free, woolen stockings, stout calfskin boots that cover the legs to the knee, well saturated with beeswax and tallow, and an India-rubber satchel for necessary toilet materials.*

Lossing also noted that women were beginning to find more pleasure and health in the wilderness than at fashionable watering places. Women seem to have become occasional climbers of Mount Marcy by the mid-1860s, though sportsmen tried to scare them off with accounts of hardships, such as the ferocious black fly. Lucia Pychowska, who climbed with her brother, Eugene Cook, and a friend, wrote in the *Continental Monthly* in December 1864: "We had heard so much of this pest, and seen so little of him, that we began to think his existence somewhat mythical, in short, a traveler's tale, invented by men to keep women from venturing beyond the well-beaten track of ordinary journeying."

Pychowska's is the earliest known magazine article about an Adirondack climb authored by a woman. Perhaps she reflected the true feelings of Marianna and Helen and the others when she wrote, "There had been no

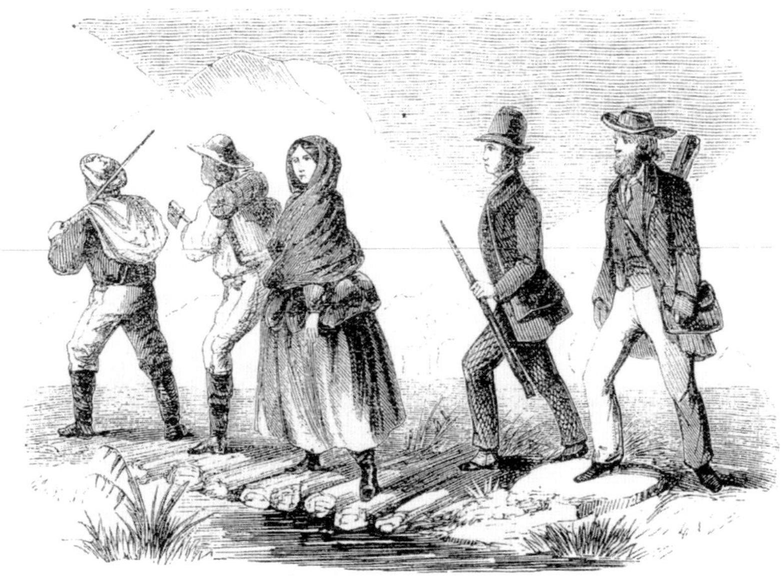

Departure for Tahawus, 1859. *Drawn by Benson J. Lossing.*

fatigue and no difficult climbing. Indeed, it would be no very serious matter to go one day and return the next. And hence we advise all travelers in that region with sound lungs, moderate strength and any love for forest life and magnificent scenery, to make the ascent."

For hiking, Pychowska recommended broad, thick-soled, low-heeled boots of soft leather, woolen stockings, an underskirt made of gray flannel and hemmed just below the knee and an outer skirt of winsey, or Kentucky jean. In places of unusual steepness, where a temporary shortening of the dress was required, "a strong clasp pin, easily carried, will in a moment fasten up the outer skirt, wash-woman fashion."

The Pychowska party—with Phelps as one of its guides—struck into the pathway to Mount Marcy for a short distance and then came to a halt near a little stream, deciding it would be a lovely spot to camp.

The next morning, the hikers looked up toward the mountaintops, and Phelps shook his head ominously. "Indeed," he said, "it won't be much use to go on up, for the Haystack looks so blue that durn'd haze must have come back again, and you'll have no view from Mercy today." The group decided nonetheless to continue up the mountain.

They crossed the little stream, climbed a half mile and came to the foot of the great slide, which rose a thousand vertical feet out of Panther Gorge. Up this slide they went and over the last steep cliffs to the summit.

"Here we are among the clouds," wrote Pychowska, "the wind blowing freshly, and the mists sweeping past, obscuring every object below...[W]hen the clouds all rolled away, and left us with bright sunlight and the most glorious view our eyes had ever rested upon. An infinity of peaks of every possible form, all gathered about us as doing homage to the stately monarch, the comely and benignant giant, Tahawus."

In 1869, William H.H. Murray's book *Adventures in the Wilderness* brought throngs of people to the Adirondacks, including women (Murray's wife had camped out in the wilderness and rode astride a horse to the top of Whiteface Mountain). In Keene Valley, vacationing ladies came to church in "daring ankle length skirts and tin cups on their belts, making tinkling sounds as they took their seats," observed Blanche Isham in *The History of the Keene Valley Congregational Church*. Many of these women came to climb Mount Marcy, but few shared Pychowska's respect for the natural world.

"Women, some women, never ought to come into the woods," remarked Old Mountain Phelps. "There was a lot of 'em I took up Mercy last summer, went gigglin' all the way up, talking of their beaux, and ribbons, and when they got up didn't see nothing. I wanted to kick 'em off the mounting."

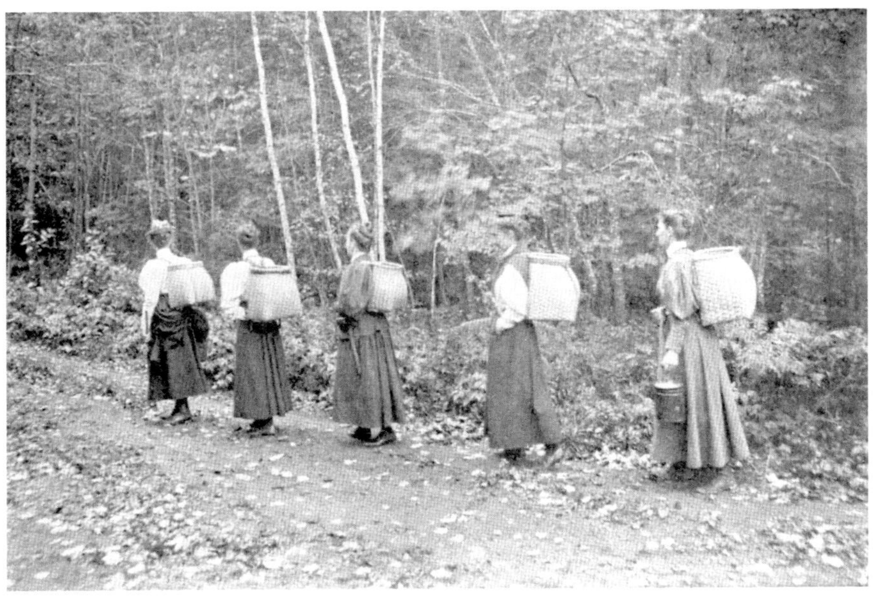

On the trail. *Photo by Katherine McClellan.*

In the 1870s, Phelps led "an eccentric lady tourist" and her companion—he nicknamed them Miss Sundry and Miss Slow—up the mountain. The pair required guides, packmen and waiters—seven in all.

Phelps described Miss Sundry as "an enthusiastic admirer of nature's wildest scenery, in her peculiar way, and she is now ready to take a trip to enjoy it." The entourage marched over brooks and fallen treetops, when "Oh! Help me up!" was heard. Phelps looked around and saw Miss Sundry sitting in a mud pool. "It was a little place of mud and water," recalled Phelps, "the water perhaps three or four inches deep and then black soft mud as deep as any reasonable person could ask for, for an easy place to sit." But Miss Sundry was calling a man to help her—this was something new, as she had made no bones about her dislike of men. Phelps sprang to her and hauled her out.

About 1870, another so-called eccentric lady tried to purchase the top of Mount Marcy from Thomas and Armstrong Lumber Company of Plattsburgh. Miss Kate Field, an internationally known journalist, author, actress and reformer, was told by Mr. Thomas that "he could only sell it to her on condition that she would make it a permanent residence, which she declining to do the trade fell through."

Regardless, Kate Field continued to encourage those women "willing to be tanned, freckled, and even made to resemble antique statuary," to try the wilderness. "Helter skelter, off with silks, kid gloves, and linen collars, on with bloomer, stout boots, and felt hat, and we helpless women are transformed into helpful human beings," she said.

In the case of Lucy Bohrman and her troupe of ladies, that helter-skelter transformation took place along the trail in 1896. The group successfully climbed Mount Marcy but had trouble on the way down. Bohrman wrote: "They did march down, down, down, over a trail so very crooked that a cat with a knot tied in its tail would have had great difficulty in getting through it. Then again it reminded of the darning process, for it was, over a log, and under a log, over a log and under a log."

Finally, one lady in the party sat down on a large rock and, using a jackknife, "with the practiced hand of one used to doing horrible things, she began to cut and slash with a ruthless hand. When she had finished, her dress was at least ten inches shorter than when she began. The remains of that dress were tenderly wound around a huge rock in the middle of the stream and left, a mute witness of the struggles which she had passed through."

Once unfettered from their fashions, nineteenth-century women loved the freedom of forest life, the thrill of magnificent scenery, the smoke of a smudge fire. "The busy, confined life of a city seemed an absurdity; the woods the only rational place for human beings to dwell in," wrote Pychowska, "and spruce boughs the only bed suitable to the dignity of mankind." Womankind, too.

Skirting the Issue

Imagine a time when women could show no athletic vigor or adventurous spirit. Not even bicycle riding was allowed for fear it would ruin the "feminine organs of matrimonial necessity" and destroy "feminine symmetry and poise."

Then

Despite the sneers and jeers of nineteenth-century society, some women went mountain hiking. Helen Lossing climbed 5,344-foot Mount Marcy in 1859. Amazingly, she completed the task clad in a stout flannel dress, a stiff petticoat, woolen stockings, high boots saturated with beeswax and a hooded cape.

Mrs. Lossing sewed loops and buttons onto her dress so that in places of unusual steepness she could temporarily shorten the length. It was also said to be "a good habit of the ladies in the Adirondacks to wear pretty hunting knives or daggers in their girdles."

Now

A hike up Mount Marcy in the twenty-first century is a bit different. Women complete the challenge as readily as men, without daggers or girdles. Most are outfitted in polypropylene shirts, microfiber shorts and Gore-Tex™ boots. Most—but not me.

To feel the experience of early female hikers, I sewed an 1860s-style dress and petticoat. Then, I set out for the summit of Mount Marcy. As expected, there were some sneers and a few stumbles on the dress hem, alleviated by clasping the skirt washwoman fashion. But there were no great difficulties. Quite the contrary; I felt the bliss of the summit breeze billowing up my skirt.

Then I had the urge to pee. I hoisted my dress, and for the first time, I did my business in the woods with "feminine symmetry and poise."

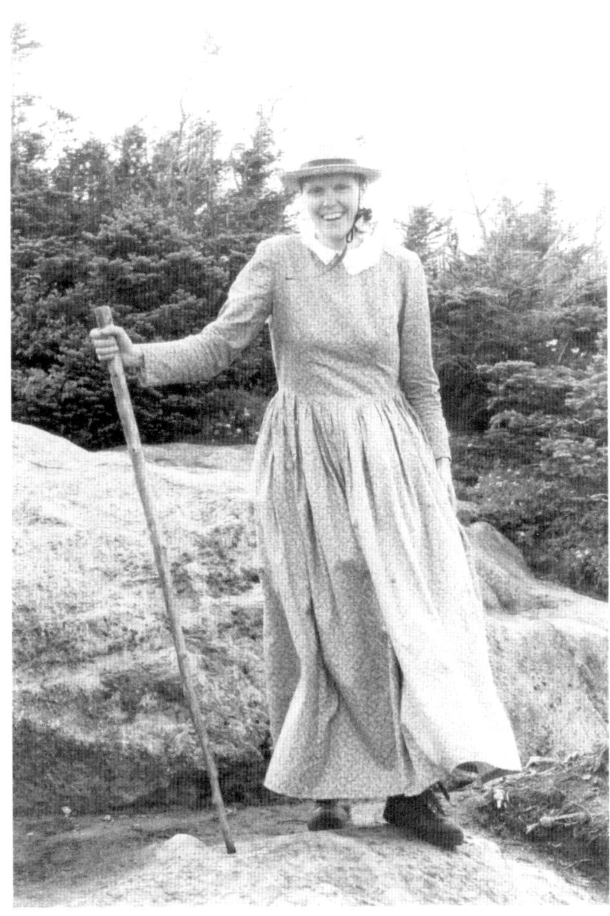

Sandra Weber hiking in handmade dress near the summit of Mount Marcy.

Grace Hudowalski, Forty-Sixer #9

Some people come into our lives and quickly go.
Some stay for a time, and leave footprints on our hearts.
And we are never, ever the same.
—Quote read at Grace's memorial service, March 21, 2004

Grace Hudowalski was a champion of the Adirondack Mountains. She was a mountaineer, mouthpiece and motherly sage, often repeating her words of wisdom: "Mountains can give you a lot if you can take it."

She was the first woman to climb all forty-six Adirondack high peaks and only the ninth person overall. She was the first president of the Adirondack Forty-Sixers, and as the club's one and only historian, she answered hundreds of letters from hikers every year. They reported to her about their climbs of each peak, and she responded by sharing personal reminiscences, inspiring the hikers to appreciate the scenes along the way and encouraging the next climb. She also promoted the region through her dynamic writing and storytelling.

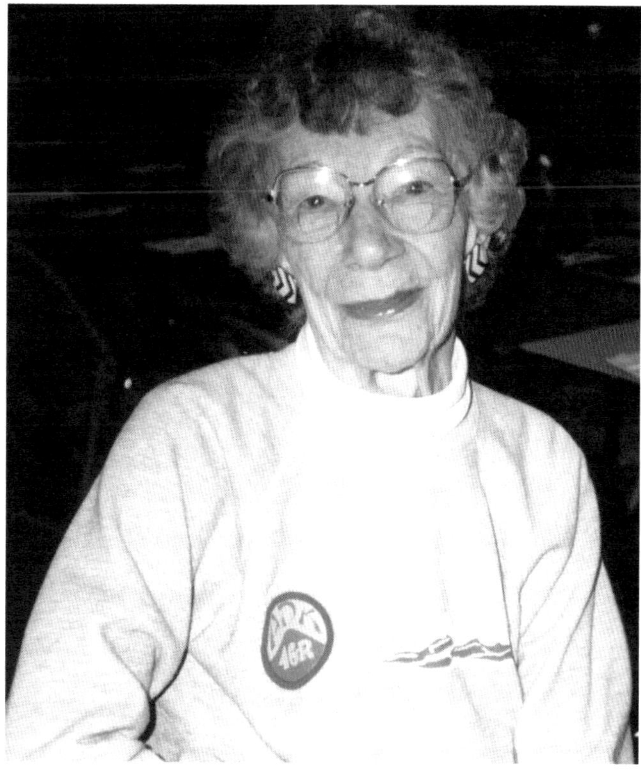

Grace Hudowalski. *Courtesy of L. John Van Norden.*

Perhaps more than any other single person, Grace represented the ideals of Adirondack hiking.

The Leach family came to America in 1629 on the first ship after the Pilgrims. Almost three centuries later, on February 26, 1906, Grace Dolbeck Leach was born in Ticonderoga. She was the baby of the family, having four older sisters and one older brother. It wasn't long before her sister Nora taught her a tough lesson.

When Grace was in second grade, Nora told her she wouldn't pass. At the end of the year, Grace didn't pass. From that experience, she learned that telling people they will fail might make them fail. "Can't never did anything" became her motto.

Another personal struggle faced Grace when she was eleven. Her mother died of cancer. Four years later, the family moved to Minerva, where her father had bought the Mountain View House. Grace said, "He had a wanderlust about him." He was always fixing up a place and then moving on; Grace didn't like moving.

During her time in Minerva, Grace discovered the Adirondack Mountains. One day in the summer of 1922, Alice Jones, of Minerva, decided to get together a group of twenty or so friends to visit Lake Colden and climb Mount Marcy. It would be a tough three-day journey, but everyone was excited.

Most of the climbers were college students, but Grace, who was only a teenager, was invited too. She begged her father to let her go, and he consented. "My bedroll was ready days ahead of time…and I was continually slipping it over my shoulder to get the feel of it," Grace recalled. "My voluminous bloomers were carefully pressed; my middy blouse, complete with the large red square of a tie (twice the size of today's kerchief), hung in readiness on a hanger."

Before she left, her father passed on some advice. He told her to do her share and more, and to do it with good cheer because "no one wants a grouch around." He also told her to walk softly and reverently. "It is not important whether you reach the top of the mountain," he said, "but it is important how you make the climb."

So young Grace Leach went off with the others to climb Mount Marcy. They arrived at the old ironworks in midafternoon and set off down the trail toward Flowed Lands. "The woods were lovely!" wrote Grace.

Clinton West, the fire ranger, met them at the water's edge and rowed them and their gear across the lake. They reached the camp on Lake Colden just before sunset. The men shared a large lean-to, and the young women slept in the ranger's cabin. Despite a cloudy sky in the morning, the group left for Mount Marcy. A drizzling rain soon began to fall. The trail was very rough and very steep in places, and the rain made the rocks and roots slippery. From Feldspar lean-to to Lake Tear of the Clouds was a tough stretch for young Grace. "My legs ached: if only I could sit down!" she wrote. "Perspiration ran down my face and black flies tormented me…Between catching breaths I asked myself, 'Why did I ever come?'"

At Four Corners lean-to, several of the party turned back. Grace had three choices: she could wait in the cold at Four Corners, she could turn back down the mountain or she could go on. "[W]ithout realizing it I was face to face with a fundamental of life," wrote Grace. She thought about her father's words—"it is important how you make the climb"—and then decided to push on toward the top.

That August day, Grace never gave up. She reached the summit on all fours, crawling like a dog, feeling her way through the soupy fog. "Everything else was forgotten but the fact I had reached the summit," she said.

Ever since that climb up Marcy, the mountains consumed her. She talked about them and wrote about them and even gave a speech about them in school.

Grace moved to Troy to live with her sister and attend high school. All members of the Leach family were teachers, except for Grace's father, but Grace never wanted to be a teacher. She took business and writing courses. She got a job as a secretary, but she made a "lousy secretary," she said. For example, she never took a class on filing systems; she created her own.

On Sundays, Grace attended the Methodist church in Troy and led a class of twelve- to fourteen-year-old girls. When the girls held a Halloween party, a friend of a friend invited Ed Hudowalski, an engineering student at Rensselaer Polytechnic Institute. Ed liked Grace immediately, but Grace was warned not to bother with him because he never dated a girl twice. Besides, the two young people had nothing in common. She was English and quiet; he was Polish and very outgoing.

Everyone was surprised when Ed proposed to Grace on their first date. "We were married forty years," Grace said.

Grace kept talking about the mountains, and finally Ed had heard enough. In 1932, he went to climb Mount Marcy and came back with a love of the mountains. By the mid-1930s, the couple had begun climbing the high peaks in earnest. Ed sometimes hiked with the minister of his Troy church, Reverend Ernest Ryder. The two men climbed their forty-sixth peak together in 1936, becoming the sixth and seventh persons to accomplish the feat. They decided it might be fun to have a social club for people who

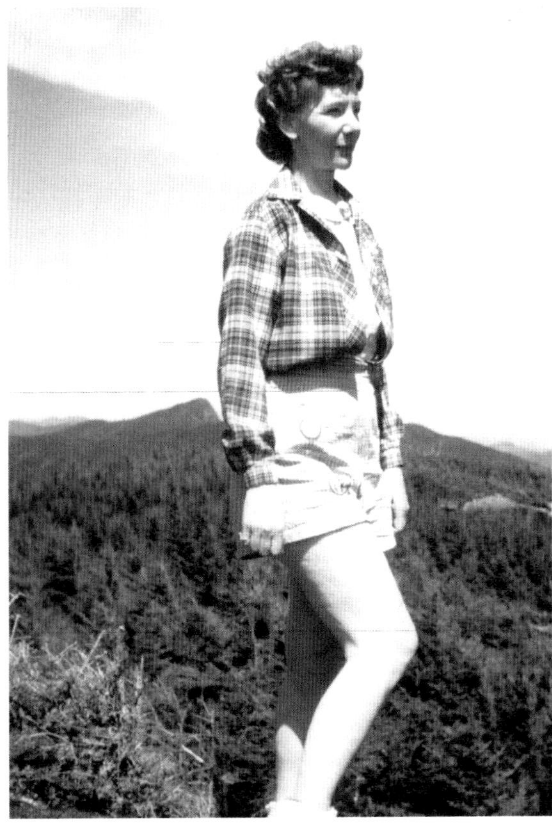

Grace Hudowalski, Forty-Sixer #9, on Phelps Mountain, 1940. *Courtesy of L. John Van Norden.*

enjoyed climbing Adirondack high peaks, so they formed the Forty-Sixers of Troy. Members had to promise to climb one mountain a year.

Grace kept climbing and soon became the first woman to climb the forty-six peaks. She finished on Mount Esther on August 26, 1937, and became Forty-Sixer #9. Tall, long-legged Grace epitomized the image of a mountain woman: sharp-witted, independent and expressive. The Forty-Sixers of Troy elected her as president from 1940 to 1942.

Grace started keeping a record of those climbing the forty-six—"for my own interest," she said. She needed some way to organize the climbers, so she devised a method. The climbers would be ordered by date and time of completing their forty-sixth peak and then alphabetically. Herb Clark was Forty-Sixer #1, George Marshall was #2 and Robert Marshall was #3 (since they had finished together and thus must be ordered by name).

By 1944, thirty people had completed the round of forty-six peaks. Grace knew that the club had to be more than a Troy group, so in 1948, the club became the Adirondack Forty-Sixers. Grace was elected the first president. The new club required members to have climbed all forty-six peaks. As for rules and regulations, Grace said, "we created rules when an occasion occurred."

Climbing has changed a bit since Grace's early climbs. Hikers didn't have frame packs or water bladders or cellphones back then. They didn't have any equipment; they used whatever they had, Grace said. They used men's work shoes as hiking boots, and the men carried supplies in pack baskets. They drank water from the streams. Grace carried a canteen once but didn't like the juggling of the water, so she never carried another canteen. Later, she started carrying a thermos of tea. The blue-checkered shorts she wore on many hikes are on display at the Adirondack Museum.

The trails were different in the mid-1900s, too. Many of the trail-less mountains did not have wide herd paths. "Let it be said here and now that trailless climbing is not child's play," she wrote in 1939. "It sounds easy enough, but following an elusive game trail, an overgrown lumber road, a winding brook, pushing through slash, falling in holes, panting up moss-covered rock ledges and, at times, even climbing a tree—these can be tough work."

Grace insisted that she never got lost—there were just lots of times when she didn't know where she was. She was never good at reading topographic maps or using a compass. "Never paid much attention to the compass," she said. Others in the group sometimes had a compass, but Grace usually just kept going. Sometimes she had to climb a tree to tell if she was headed in the right direction.

During World War II, Ed was called away to serve in the Signal Corps of the United States Army. He traveled overseas to England, Italy, India, China and other places. Back home, Grace worked for Social Services as a stenographer—"a lousy stenographer," she said.

Grace wrote many articles for Adirondack Mountain Club magazines and newsletters and for the Forty-Sixers. But she had never been a paid writer until the Conservation Department asked her to be a publicity writer. She took the job, and then, just a month later, she went to the Commerce Department. From 1945 to 1961, she worked as a travel promotion writer, popular storyteller and radio personality. To her surprise, her salary soared to $3,100. "I was earning twice as much as my husband!" Grace boasted.

In 1953, Ed and Grace bought a camp on the east shore of Schroon Lake. Grace spent every summer and many other vacation days or weekends at the Boulders. Hikers were always welcome to drop in and share stories of their adventures. Grace would listen with great interest, often sipping on her favorite drink, a "bastard daiquiri" made with dark rum and a dash of bottled mix.

In the 1960s and 1970s, hikers came under criticism as "peakbaggers," climbing for the sake of speed records and disregarding the pristine surroundings. While there are some who deserved that label, Grace certainly did not. As Laura and Guy Waterman pointed out in *Forest and Crag*, "No one could dream of accusing her of failing to appreciate the mountains."

The Forty-Sixers adopted stewardship programs to "give something back" to the mountains. Grace welcomed new hikers with this message: "We hope that you will join the Forty-Sixers in a growing stewardship for the high peaks. May you have many enjoyable, safe and responsible trips in these mountains. Good climbing!"

Grace continued her love affair with the mountains after Ed passed away in 1966. At the age of seventy, she decided to reclimb the peaks even though her doctor didn't think it was a good idea since she had just broken two ribs. Ten years later, at age eighty, she decided to climb Cascade Mountain. A doctor had told her to walk with a cane, she said, but he didn't tell her not to climb.

At age ninety-one, Grace rode up the Whiteface Memorial Highway and climbed the final steps to the summit to celebrate the sixtieth anniversary of her completion of the forty-six high peaks. To honor Grace, hikers climbed to the summits of the other forty-five peaks that day. Some waved flags and blew whistles; others picked blueberries for her.

One sad note in Grace's life was that health issues prevented her from having children. Instead, she made the Forty-Sixers her family; she became the matron of mountaineers. For decades, she corresponded with every aspiring and accomplished Forty-Sixer, writing more than sixteen hundred letters some years. Through this simple (albeit time-consuming) act, Grace compelled hikers to do more than just run to the summit. She made them reflect on what they saw along the way, who climbed with them and how the experience made them feel.

At age ninety, Grace finally gave up the letter writing. The job is now attempted by a committee of several people who marvel at how Grace did her job—and without the aid of a computer.

"Grace dedicated her life to helping others follow the trail of the first Forty-Sixers, guiding, educating and entertaining each climber in the Forty-Sixer pursuit," says L. John Van Norden, Forty-Sixer #2110. "Her tales of those early days are legendary and have always been an inspiration."

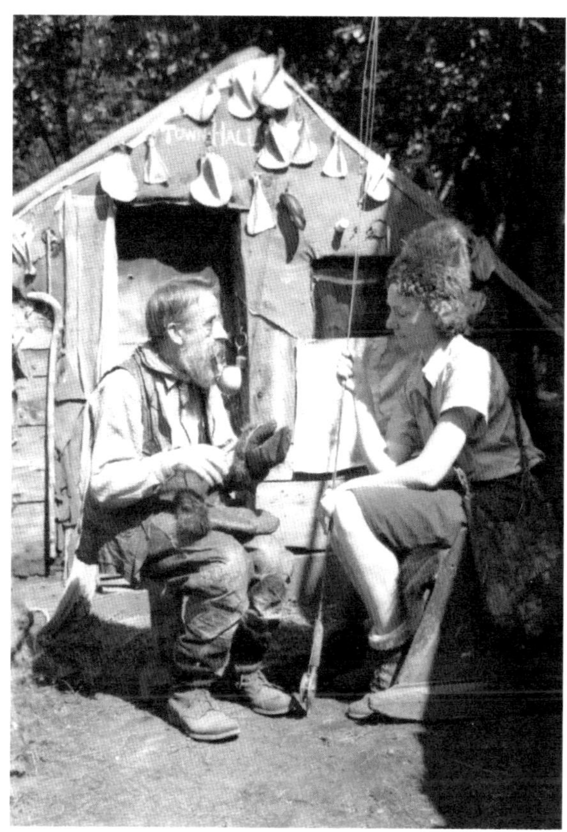

Grace Hudowalski with hermit Noah John Rondeau at Cold River. *Courtesy of L. John Van Norden.*

The Adirondack Forty-Sixers captured some of Grace's tales on a CD in 2001. *Mountain Tales by Grace* contains many fascinating stories about snakes, trap dikes, naked hikers and hermit Noah John Rondeau. It also explains Grace's most unusual experience: waking up in a lean-to next to a man she hadn't seen in years.

Even when Grace could no longer climb the peaks, she continued to find ways to touch them. Using her own money, she created the Adirondack 46R Conservation Trust, an independent charitable endowment. In May 2000, she generated additional funds for the trust by auctioning her Hudowalski Adirondackana Collection. More than six hundred items were sold, including a private copy of Robert Marshall's *Doonerak or Bust*, a signed copy of Verplanck Colvin's 1873 Survey Report and a Rockwell Kent book inscribed to Grace with a pen drawing of Whiteface Mountain. The trust's mission is to preserve the "forever wild" character of the Adirondack High Peaks region through education and conservation. The trust cares for the peaks in many ways, including helping to fund the Summit Steward Program, a program critical to preserving the fragile alpine vegetation atop some of the high peaks.

On March 13, 2004, just days after her ninety-eighth birthday, Grace passed away. She gave her time and energy to the mountains, and her contributions will benefit the Adirondacks for decade upon decade.

Her legacy has been widely recognized. The Adirondack Mountain Club presented her with its highest honor, the Trail Blazer Award, in 2004. There is also an effort under way by the Adirondack Forty-Sixers to have a mountain honor Grace. The head of the Grace Peak committee, Doug Arnold, said, "Grace created a family of mountain climbers in the Adirondacks. She drew us together and inspired people to keep climbing." Now the climbers intend to petition the federal government to officially change the name of East Dix to Grace Peak as a tribute to Grace Hudowalski. Many hikers, and Forty-Sixers, have already started calling the 4,012-foot mountain Grace Peak. The Forty-Sixers hope that having the new name become the commonly used name will help persuade the government to accept Grace Peak.

It would seem quite fitting for Grace and Esther to be the only two high peaks named for women, both of whom climbed for the sheer joy of climbing.

Forest Studies

The Big Burn

A Century Ago, a Half-Million Acres Went Up in Smoke

In the early spring of 1903, there were no signs of trouble, no indications of the dire drought and horrendous fires that would ravage the Adirondacks. In March, Lake Champlain was at its highest level in memory. Two months later, the water would drop thirty-three inches.

April and May were usually dangerous months for fires, according to William F. Fox, superintendent of New York State Forests in 1903. That time of year, the snow had melted and the green leaves were not out yet. The ground was covered with dead leaves and piles of brush from logging, which made abundant, extremely dry fuel. A single ember from a smoking pipe, a campfire left smoldering or a spark from a locomotive was enough to light the tinder, and a strong breeze could quickly spread the flames.

A few fires early in 1903 were quickly extinguished. Still, the April rains did not come, and dry winds raked the region. Incipient fires sprang up, from Lake Placid to Elizabethtown to Long Lake, Old Forge, Cranberry Lake, Tupper Lake and the St. Regis Lakes.

Fires were common near railroad lines in the wake of freight and passenger trains. By the end of April, burns broke out along the tracks of the New York Central, the Chateaugay, the New York & Ottawa and the Saranac & Lake Placid Railroads. Fire warden C.W. Rowe reported that the engines on the Delaware & Hudson Railroad set fires on the mountain south of Port Kent nearly every day.

A law specified that locomotives used in the woods must have steel netting or screens to prevent sparks from escaping. Railroad authorities knew of the danger but continued to run engines without screens. The only penalty was a $100 fine—not much of a deterrent for wealthy railroad companies.

Ella Flagg of Saranac Lake reported that an engine named Grace set a fire and ruined much of her property. She said, "It would have burned our cottage only for myself and daughter fighting fire until the fire department arrived."

W.K. Benedict traveled on the New York Central from Saranac Lake to New York City. While standing in the last car, he observed, "At very frequent intervals the tracks in the rear of the train were strewn with live coals, dumped from the locomotive, and in many instances these coals, dropping on the wooden ties, burned into bright flames, which only required a slight breeze to spread to the side of the tracks and to the forest."

As the number of fires grew, there simply were not enough local people to handle the situation. The New York Central sent carloads of Italian laborers to help fight fires along the company's line. Even with the extra help, conditions worsened, and on May 7, some freight runs were temporarily discontinued in hopes that rain would soon relieve the drought.

However, trains were not the only problem. Farmers burned brush to clear fields. Laws forbade farmers to kindle fallow fields between April 1 and June 1 because of dry conditions. Not everyone obeyed; fallow burns were the second leading cause of forest fires in 1903. Wardens fined fifty-six offenders and collected more than $1,700 in fines.

Fishermen and tobacco smokers caused blazes. Hunters, wintergreen pickers, incendiaries and sparks from chimneys were blamed in a few cases. Fires were also started by wind-whipped sparks from other fires.

Superintendent Fox noted other odd causes: "lunatic, dooryard fire, children at play, smoking out a hedgehog, burning a straw bed, burning ferns, blasting stone, sparks from torch and lightning." Some blazes were allegedly set by men in order to gain employment, but Fox reported that "no evidence whatever has been furnished thus far in support of that theory."

The law made no provision for paying fire wardens and their men for patrolling or preventing fires. They were only paid for time spent fighting blazes. Whenever a fire broke out, wardens hired a gang and set them to work. During the spring of 1903, 6,487 men were conscripted to fight fires.

The wardens used a variety of methods to control the fires. Surface fires were stopped by raking the leaf litter. The crews used water if they could find it. At Inlet, men carried water by hand until they were able to connect

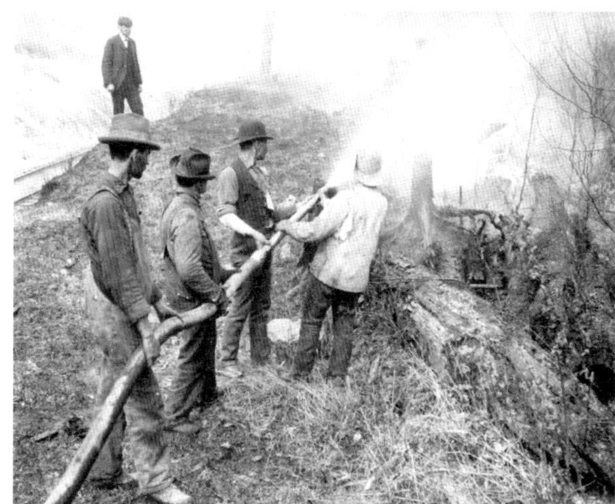

Right: New York Central Railroad fire crew, 1903. *Courtesy of the Adirondack Museum.*

Below: Nehasane Park Fire Service crew, 1903. *Courtesy of the Adirondack Museum.*

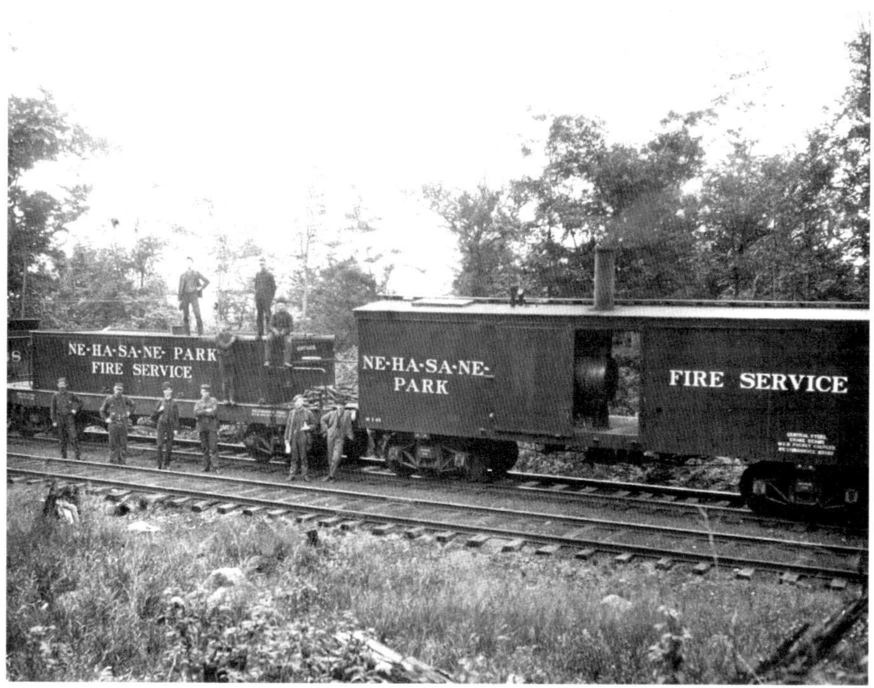

a pipeline and turn a one-and-one-half-inch stream of water on the burning ground. But water sources were not always available, as reported by a fire warden in Fulton County: "The fire is still burning in the ground at places. It cannot be extinguished now, as there is no water."

The manager at Dr. W. Seward Webb's Nehasane Preserve in Hamilton County resorted to extraordinary measures; he invited scientist and inventor Carl E. Meyers to bring his "explosive balloon" to cause artificial precipitation.

At times, men set backfires or plowed ditches to keep fires from spreading. They also used shovels to dig trenches. Dry duff made it necessary to dig the trench from one to four feet wide and down to the mineral soil. In St. Huberts, 250 men dug a trench to encircle the town completely and save it.

Women helped, too. A.N. Skiff, from Onchiota, wrote, "The women fought two nights, all night long, and waded brooks clear to their knees. I say they fought fire better than the men, they were that scared, and were more thorough in putting it out than the men were."

On April 30, high winds quickly spread the flames. The *New York Times* reported, "Nothing but a good long rain will save the woods in many places…Telephone and telegraph wires are down, and but few details are at hand to-night, but enough is known to make it certain that the worst forest fire in years is raging."

Dangerous conditions continued through the month of May, which was the driest in seventy-seven years. The wardens and firefighters worked fifteen hours a day, week after week, sometimes camping in the woods near the fires. Reports of fires kept coming. The Hurd sawmill at Tupper Lake, the largest in the country when it was erected, caught fire and was destroyed. A thousand acres burned near the site of Fort Gate, south of Lake George. Chazy Lake, Standish, Schuyler Falls and Keene all reported fires.

"Yesterday was a terrible day here, and I never wish to see the like again," wrote W. Scott Brown from St. Huberts. "Fire came over the Giant [Mountain] about 11 a.m. yesterday with a strong wind. Some say the flames went 200 ft. high…Wind was high and air filled with firey [*sic*] pieces of wood, bark, etc…It took the grit out of some people here quick."

In nearby Euba Mills, on the Boquet River, an old sawmill burned, and the Proctor family barely escaped with the clothing on their backs. In an adjacent stream, men found hundreds of dead brown trout weighing up to two pounds. The *Elizabethtown Post* asked, "What killed these trout, extreme heat, lye, lime, oil or fright?"

The top of St. Regis Mountain was burning; at Dannemora, crews were keeping watch on the prison. Other state property was in danger in North Elba. Reuben Lawrence, custodian of the John Brown Farm historic site, reported that fires were near the farm and state lands. "The men are doing all they can to keep it from the house…We are living in hopes that God will send rain…All the men in this town are tired out and sick and exhausted. Still they will have to work."

Areas far removed from the flames witnessed the effects. Smoke from the Adirondacks settled over New York City and caused a "yellow day." The *New York Times* reported that grass and flowers in Central Park "looked as if they had been daubed with yellow paint, owing to the peculiar reflection due to the smoke." In Lake George, ash fell like a heavy snowfall, and in Utica, noted the *Times*, "the sun did not cast a shadow, but hung like a red ball in the heavens."

By June, the situation grew desperate. In North Elba, brush left from lumbering made good fuel, and fires swept over ten thousand acres in one afternoon. At Heart Lake, Henry Van Hoevenberg's Adirondack Lodge and fourteen other buildings were destroyed. Somehow the flames spared one flimsy bark shelter, which contained a half box of dynamite. Van Hoevenberg made a brave move; he stuffed the dynamite under his coat, ran across the smoldering ground to the lake and tossed the explosives into the water.

Along the shore of Heart Lake lay fish that had been cooked to death. The same thing had happened in the inlet of Big Moose Lake, where the fierce heat of a fire raised the water temperature.

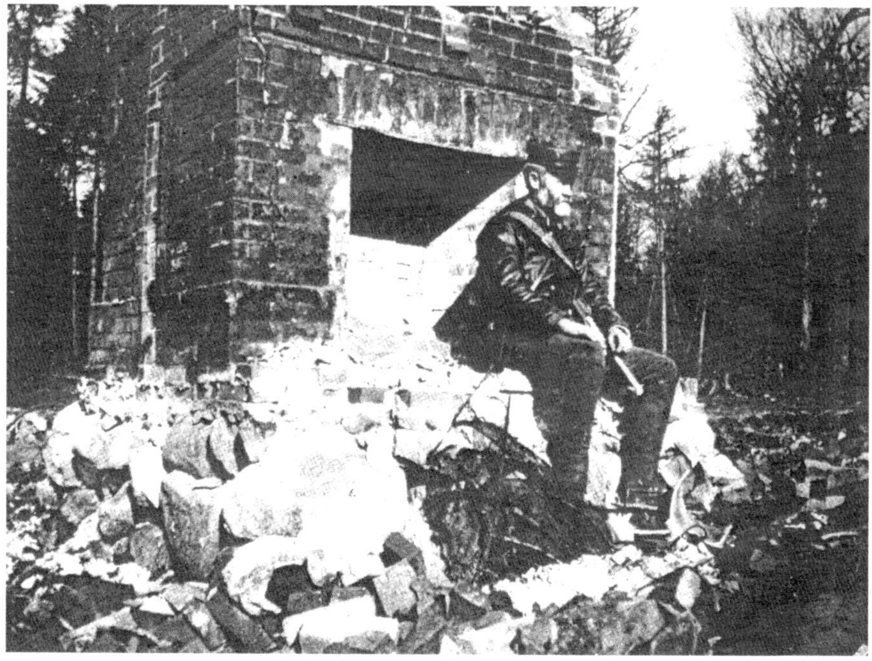

Henry Van Hoevenberg in rubble of the fire of 1903.

The road between Lake Placid and Saranac Lake was filled with snakes, rabbits, porcupines and deer that had been scared out of the blazing woods. The *Elizabethtown Post* reported that many dead deer were found in the ruined forests. "Some of these deer were badly burned, some appeared to be only slightly scorched and some bore no fire marks. Query: Do deer sometimes die of fright, pure and simple?"

Relief came on June 7 as rain fell on the region. Hundreds of men dropped their tools that day. The six weeks of firefighting were over.

People celebrated and gave thanks for the rain. And the showers kept coming. Near Keene, rain continued for twenty-four hours, and it certainly did lots of good, but then it became too much. Streams rose until they flooded. An iron bridge and several wooden bridges were washed away, and landslides cut off roads. "What next? It seems as though Fate were against us," wrote W. Scott Brown.

By the time the fires were extinguished, about 464,000 acres burned in the Adirondack forest, according to Superintendent Fox. He estimated that more than $800,000 had been lost in timber, logs, pulpwood and property.

But according to the report by forester H.M. Suter for the United States Department of Agriculture, "over 600,000 acres of timberland in northern New York were burned over," and the direct loss was approximately $3.5 million. This document explained that the accurate determination of the losses "is an impossibility." Reported losses were just over $1 million, but that number was known to understate the damage, so it was modified.

How could there be such a discrepancy? Suter's estimates included the region of "northern New York," while Fox examined the Adirondack lands, which meant looking at each county and determining how much of the damage was actually inside the Adirondack Park. (The park in 1903 was about half its current size.) It also appears that the state was trying to minimize the disaster.

In a *New York Times* article, the Forestry Department reported that burns were much less extensive than previously stated, and the loss of virgin timber had been exaggerated. Fox told the *Times*, "The Summer visitor will see no changes in the woods as he looks out upon them from the hotels, cottages and camps." The article explained the department's motivation for such a statement: "The Forestry Department is interested in the maintenance of Summer business in the Adirondacks."

Local newspapers and officials also tried to assure tourists that the scenic beauty had "not been marred in the least." The *Elizabethtown Post* blamed New York City papers for "overdrawing the fire picture" to sell more copies. "One unacquainted with the actual condition of things here would think…

that there wasn't anything left to look at but black fire tracts," claimed the *Post*. "However, such is not the fact…There is not a single black fire track visible from this village."

That wasn't true, either. Certainly, the destruction of Euba Mills marred the scene, and the blackened summit of Giant loomed near Elizabethtown. Tourists taking the fashionable hike up Mount Marcy were in for a shock, too. "We had never seen anything like it. For mile after mile, there was nothing but charred blackness," noted one hiker. "Every bit of the Marcy trail was burned away, as was the forest floor covering of leaves, duff and everything else."

The *Post* article was correct that there had been exaggerations. Reports claimed that the fires caused several fatalities; they hadn't caused any. Other reports overstated the danger faced by the grand hotels. The only significant building destroyed was the Adirondack Lodge.

As a result of the fires, authorities tried unsuccessfully to persuade railroad companies to convert their wood- and coal-burning locomotives to oil. Loggers and residents were asked to help prevent the careless and criminal use of fire. However, Suter felt improvements to the fire patrol system must be made. He said, "Should another long drought occur, the state would be powerless under present methods against fire to prevent a repetition of the calamity."

Despite Suter's warnings, new methods and improvements to fire services did not come fast enough. When another drought hit in 1908, fires raged through the region. Not until 1909 were measures taken, including establishment of a paid fire patrol, a top-lopping law requiring loggers to cut tree branches and leave them to rot and the construction of mountaintop observation towers. A test of their effectiveness came in 1911, during another drought. This time, the fire damage was limited.

Over the decades, fire patrolling moved from summits to small airplanes, and fire towers were eventually abandoned. Today, with well-trained response organizations using modern equipment like helicopters to battle occasional blazes in the forests, it is unlikely that the widespread destruction of one hundred years ago will ever happen again.

At Duck Hole

Day 10: Friday, August 8

In the morning, we find that the other campers have left, so we move our stuff to Duck Hole lean-to #2. We pitch the tent so that it will dry in the sunshine.

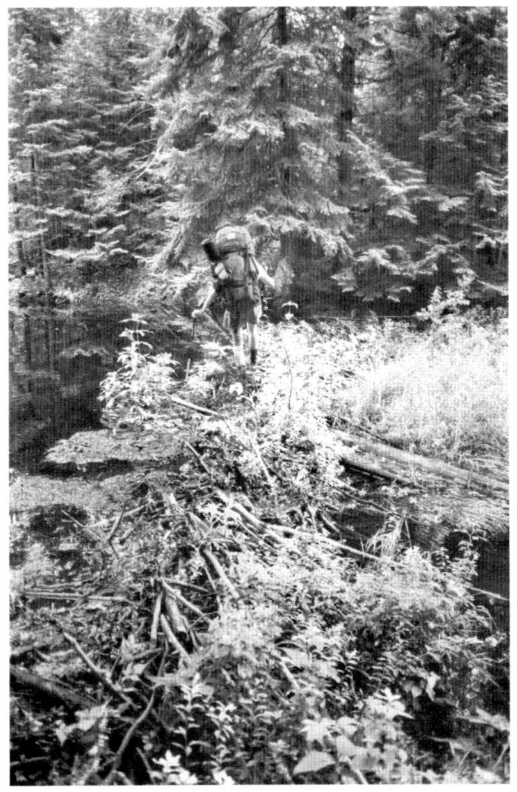

Sandra Weber walking over a beaver dam on the way to Duck Hole. *Photo by Carl Heilman.*

This spot feels remote and wild. The wind howls in the distance, and there are ragged mountain peaks. Lily pads float on the surface of the pond, and hemlocks and pines line the shore. There is plenty of company, too. Chickadees, butterflies, grasshoppers, loons, woodpeckers and ducks roam Duck Hole.

Even the outhouse is extraordinary. The sign on the door says Nat Well's Parlor of Muse. It is a strange place to sit and ponder your dreams, but the view is quite pretty. Through the open doorway, I can peek at the forest, the hills and the ripples on the pond.

To our surprise, it is a warm, sunny day. To think I almost canceled this part of the trip! And now this is the best weather yet.

We have not seen another person for hours. We have the entire world to ourselves. I go swimming in the deep pool in front of the log dam. It is wonderful to lie back and float in the water like a lily pad.

Marcy is a grasshopper in the meadow. Her long legs pounce through prickly berry bushes, with her long hair chasing behind. After her walk, she settles into the tent to read Tolkien's *The Lord of the Rings: Part II, The Two Towers*. I didn't want to bring the book; it was extra weight. But I decided to let her have this luxury. Besides, I recalled that book pages do have practical uses. In an emergency, they can be used as fire starters or as toilet paper.

In the afternoon, we decide to build a campfire. It is legal to have fires in this area of the Adirondacks. I search for dry sticks, but everything is wet from yesterday's rain. Marcy gathers birch bark to help kindle the damp wood. Working together, we manage to get a fire started.

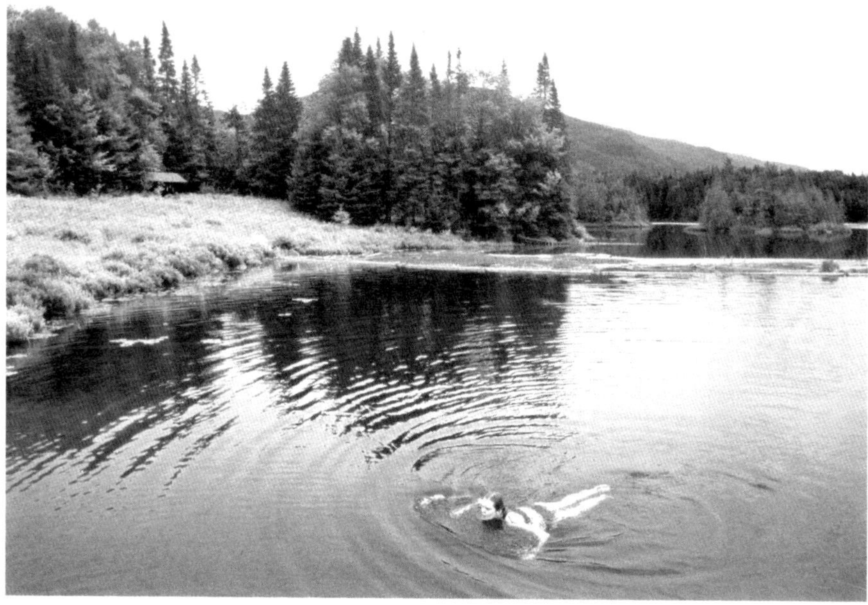

A refreshing swim at Duck Hole. *Photo by Carl Heilman.*

Later, while I am fanning the flames, a huge garter snake crawls toward the fire. I scream and run away. Marcy grabs a stick, picks up the snake and carries it into the meadow.

I come out of hiding and start to cook dinner. Just then, big booms of thunder echo off the mountains. We manage to heat our noodles before the raindrops arrive. For two hours, the thunder and lightning circle above our heads, and the rain pours down. We listen to the *drip, piddle, splat* of water dropping from the lean-to's roof into the moat that has formed around us.

As the sky finally brightens, three loons swim near our camp and announce their presence with wild calls.

After the sun sinks behind the hills, we light a candle. Its soft glow casts a brightness and warmth into the damp, dark woods. Somehow, we seem to sense that this will be our last night of camping. Neither of us wants to go to sleep. We want to make this time together last as long as we can.

Marcy reads her book by candlelight while I lie beside her and listen to the silence. Finally, we put out the candle and snuggle into our sleeping bags. Before I close my eyes, the moon peeks out of the clouds and shines on Duck Hole.

This is not a "dismal" wilderness. It is a bright and wondrous place, a place I do not want to leave.

The Peat Bog Track

The peat bog track
Goes on and on.
You wish your house were further in.
The leaf and the log,
The bee and the toad,
Help to guide you on your way.
The mountains are white.
The air's growing cold,
And you just want to say,
Keep me—past streams and weeds.
Don't let me back,
I want to learn the ways of those gone loose.
I have been penned up,
For so many years.
My brothers and sisters kept me back,
Now I travel without fear or load.
—Marcy Weber, 2003

Savior of the Summits

When this man saw the damage above timberline, his first question was: "How can we fix it?"

Silver-haired professor Edwin H. Ketchledge, dressed in blue jeans, a windbreaker and a fishing hat, blends with the camcorder-toting crowds atop Whiteface Mountain. Together, they marvel at the views of Lake Placid, Mount Marcy and the other distant peaks. "That one is Algonquin, the second highest," Ketchledge often points out to visitors.

He doesn't mention that he has climbed it 180 times. Or that he is responsible for preserving the alpine vegetation on its summit. Or that he has climbed all forty-six high peaks—those mountains over four thousand feet—despite lungs disabled by a bullet wound.

Ed Ketchledge has spent much of his life atop the Adirondacks, browsing for minute sprouts, flowers and mosses; spreading grass seed over eroded meadows; teaching others about the fragile alpine environment; and sometimes just admiring the glorious view. "My first climbs were for purely scientific reasons," he explains. "My very first climb up Algonquin was in the summer of 1949. I was exploring for mosses for my graduate work." That work led to a master's in botany, a PhD in biology and, in 1955, a position as instructor of forest botany at SUNY College of Forestry at Syracuse.

Over the next forty years, Ketchledge's reasons for mountain climbing slowly evolved. His first epiphany came in the 1960s as he stood on Algonquin admiring the ethereal view of Mount Marcy. Then he looked down at his feet surrounded by candy wrappers, tin cans, bottle caps and other garbage.

Ketchledge's concerns about littering led to "clean-up parties." Starting in 1966, hikers from the Adirondack Mountain Club (ADK) climbed Marcy to collect rubbish and haul out the trash. In an effort to keep the trails and summits clean, Ketchledge promoted the concept, "If you pack it in, pack it out!"—now a wilderness ethic nationwide.

"That trash problem triggered my ecological sensitivities," he says. He switched his research from purely scientific study to ecological study. With support from the United States Forest Service, he started an inventory of the damage to the highest Adirondack summits and began a search for ways to correct the problems.

The inventory required Ketchledge to climb all forty-six high peaks—not a simple task for any person, but for a man with lung problems, it was an extraordinary feat. His disability occurred while he served as a ski trooper with the 10th Mountain Division during World War II. After training in Colorado, he went to Italy, where he fought at Riva Ridge. Two months later, in the Apennine Mountains, Ketchledge charged out of a ravine and into machine gun fire. A bullet went through his left lung, grazed his heart and then passed through his diaphragm and stomach. He was awarded a Bronze Star and Purple Heart and was discharged 100 percent disabled.

He largely recovered, but the wound left him with reduced lung capacity and the lingering probability of heart problems. He has never forgotten his war experiences and the four soldiers who took bullets trying to help him. On July 30, 1995, Ketchledge spoke at a celebration on the top of Esther Mountain:

> *This is a special day on a special mountain for me. Half a century ago this morning, near the end of World War II, I was discharged from an army hospital...I have counted every day—one by one—since then as a reprieve, an opportunity to make my life worthwhile, a second chance not received by 992 of my buddies in the 10th Mountain Division. Today is 18,369. Every morning I get up is a blessing for me.*

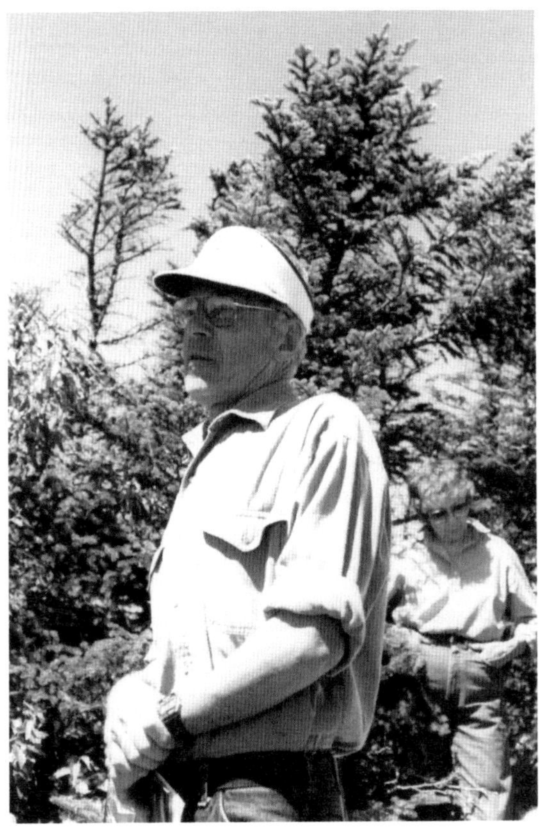

Dr. Edwin Ketchledge speaking at a celebration on Esther Mountain on July 30, 1995.

As he surveyed the high peaks in the late 1960s, Ketchledge found that the damage being done by hikers was severe. The problems had gone beyond litter to trampling. When hikers avoided rocks, wandered from the trail for a better view or sat on soft moss, they crushed vegetation and caused soil erosion.

The alpine tundra that covers the tops of the highest Adirondack mountains is rare, old and fragile. These plants have been growing on the summits since the glaciers retreated and are not usually found outside Alaska, Newfoundland or the Arctic. Twenty of the alpine species are not found any farther south than the Adirondacks.

Ketchledge was disturbed to see our natural heritage, these rare survivors of much earlier times, being destroyed. He asked himself, "How can we fix it?"

None of the scientific literature discussed how to restore alpine vegetation. That didn't stop Ketchledge. "When there is a cause, he is directed—and he acts unselfishly," says Ray Curran, a former Ketchledge student now in charge of natural-resource analysis for the Adirondack Park Agency (APA). "He received no research funds and very little credit for the pioneering work he was doing. But he knew it was important and he did it."

What he did was put his scientific skills to work and develop a method of restoring native alpine vegetation. His process paralleled that used by highway engineers to vegetate road banks. Starting on Dix Mountain in 1967, he planted several test areas and discovered that bluegrass and red fescue combined with fertilizer and lime worked best. His sole purpose was to stop the erosion by quickly producing grass, which would stabilize the surface. Once the soil was secured, he would figure out a plan to restore the native vegetation.

But Ketchledge never had to figure out that plan; nature went to work. In the next two or three years, as the common grasses died, native species of moss, liverwort and lichen began to invade the surface. The mat of mosses then provided the necessary seedbed conditions for the slow invasion of vascular plants, led by mountain sandwort and then three-toothed cinquefoil or Bigelow's sedge.

It was time to carry the method to other summits. In 1970, ADK members and Adirondack Forty-Sixers volunteered to lug eleven-pound restoration kits up the mountains. The hikers-turned-gardeners fertilized, limed and spread grass seed. As they watched the results, they discovered that the process was only successful if hikers stayed off the site. So the volunteers first picked the least damaging trail to the summit, marked it and eliminated other trails. They covered the steep sides of the trail with loose rocks and then treated the site with the grass mixture. As soon as the sod grew, it held the rocks and stabilized the banks along the trail. Most sites were treated two or three times, seasonally, in May or June.

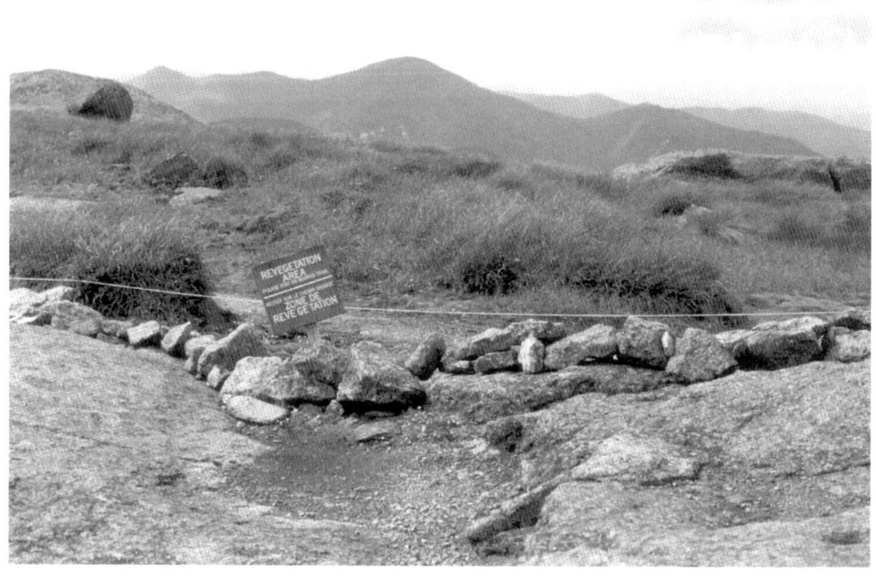

Revegetation area on Mount Marcy.

The Forty-Sixers carried on this work for twenty-seven years.

In the meantime, a new challenge arose. The number of hikers became a problem. Twenty thousand people a year visited Mount Marcy. It wasn't a matter of cleaning up after them or reseeding herd paths—it was a problem of entire mountaintops being covered with boots on summer weekends.

But Ketchledge offered the solution once again. The teacher converted the summits from playgrounds to open-air classrooms. His interest in the mountains had now progressed from scientific to ecological to educational.

In 1989, he led an effort to place naturalists on top of the two highest peaks every day throughout the summer. Their role would be to greet visitors, answer questions and talk about alpine vegetation and what hikers could do to help protect the summit environment. Ketchledge was surprised when he initially presented the idea to the Adirondack Nature Conservancy. "They gave the program $10,000 immediately," he recalls. "The Conservancy's Kathy Regan is the one who really sold the idea. She is the mother figure of the Summit Stewardship program."

Regan says there would be five stewards this summer [1999], working full time on Marcy and Algonquin and part time on Wright, Colden, Haystack and Skylight. They will probably greet fifteen thousand hikers.

With the ecological fix in place and the public education continuing, Ketchledge is optimistic. But he believes the Department of Environmental Conservation has been shirking its duty as custodian of the High Peaks. "For a decade now, private money has paid for the summit stewards," he says. "And for a quarter of a century, volunteers have done the revegetation. It's high time the state took the lead here."

Now, at age seventy-four, this teacher who has inspired two generations of students and hikers hopes to instill a sense of stewardship in thousands more atop Whiteface Mountain. In recent years, emphysema has prevented him from climbing mountains; he has only one-third of the normal flow capacity of his lungs and only one-half the normal volume. He is forced to reach the only summit he can, the only summit accessible by automobile.

He drives up the slopes of Whiteface and studies the decline of the red spruce and its possible link to acid rain. He watches the natural progress of fir waves on neighboring Esther Mountain. And, once again, he is applying his talents as educator and ecologist, this time as a founding member of the local citizen's organization called Whiteface Preservation and Resource Association.

With the cooperation of the Olympic Regional Development Authority, the group maintains an interpretive center at the tollhouse on the Whiteface highway. Ketchledge created natural history displays and a "tree trail" (where they planted and identified tree species) around nearby Stevens Pond, and he leads interpretive tours up the mountain. He hopes he can communicate his passion for the Adirondack high country to the carloads of tourists.

It is not an easy task.

While on a tour of Whiteface a few years ago, I helped Ketchledge carry stones up the mountain and place them along the banks of the walkway where erosion was occurring. As our group descended the trail in the afternoon, an excited tourist bounded down the mountain. We stared in amazement at the five-pound rock in his hand.

Someone quietly said, "Hey, you're going the wrong way." But the man didn't hear and carried the precious souvenir to his car. We shook our heads and groaned. But Ketchledge was hopeful.

"Lots of people want to help but don't know what to do. Anybody who can relate to the environment in some way—can appreciate beautiful little flowers, a tall tree, a rock—can learn anything you are willing to teach them."

Fir Waves

An ocean is a great place to watch waves. Whitecaps rise and crash onto the sandy beach. Salty spray splashes high into the air.

Do you know another exciting place to watch waves? On a mountain! It might sound ridiculous, but it's true. I like to watch waves roll up the high slopes of mountains. My favorite place is Esther Mountain.

Of course, it takes about sixty years to see the waves rise and fall, because these aren't waves of water. These are waves of trees. They occur only in pure stands of balsam fir and are called "fir waves."

From a nearby mountaintop, I look across at the evergreen forest on the upper slopes of Esther. The long, curved strips of gray, dead trees are easy to spot in the dark green forest. They *do* resemble ocean waves moving toward shore, crashing into everything in their path.

Fir waves were first noticed on mountains in Japan in the 1950s. In the 1970s, people noticed fir waves in the mountains of northeastern North America. These are the only two places in the world where fir waves are known to occur.

Naturally Wavy

At first, scientists thought pollution or some kind of disease caused the gray strips. They were surprised to discover that fir waves are part of the natural life-and-death cycle of certain high-elevation forests.

Dr. Edwin Ketchledge has studied fir waves in the Adirondack Mountains. He learned that fir waves occur at elevations above four thousand feet (1,220 meters). The trees face harsh conditions at such high elevations.

Tough Life

Imagine being pounded with bitter cold, strong winds and lots of moisture, day after day, season after season. And think about blizzards in July and August. Few trees can survive in that environment, and firs barely do.

Survival is especially difficult for trees on the western slopes of the Adirondack Mountains. Most days, the wind comes from the west. Because of this, fir waves usually occur on west-facing slopes.

Hole in the Forest

A wave begins when a few trees reach old age. They lose some branches. Ice kills needles and buds. A strong wind loosens the roots of the old, weakened trees. Soon, the trees die, and their branches and trunks turn gray.

These dead, gray trees manage to keep standing. But they are bare. They have no needles. They are like a "hole" in the green canopy that protects the forest.

A hole gives the wind a way to get into the forest. Healthy trees on the edge of the hole are now in danger. The west wind sweeps into the hole and whips uphill. Ice and snow join the attack. The row of living trees uphill from the hole of dead trees begins to lose needles and branches. They suffer root damage and soon stop growing. Slowly, they die. Their gray trunks mark the upper edge of the wave.

The next uphill row of healthy trees is now under attack. Year after year, the cycle continues up the mountainside.

A Doomed Forest?

It sounds like the whole forest is doomed. But what is happening on the *downhill* side of the wave? Where did those dead, gray trees go?

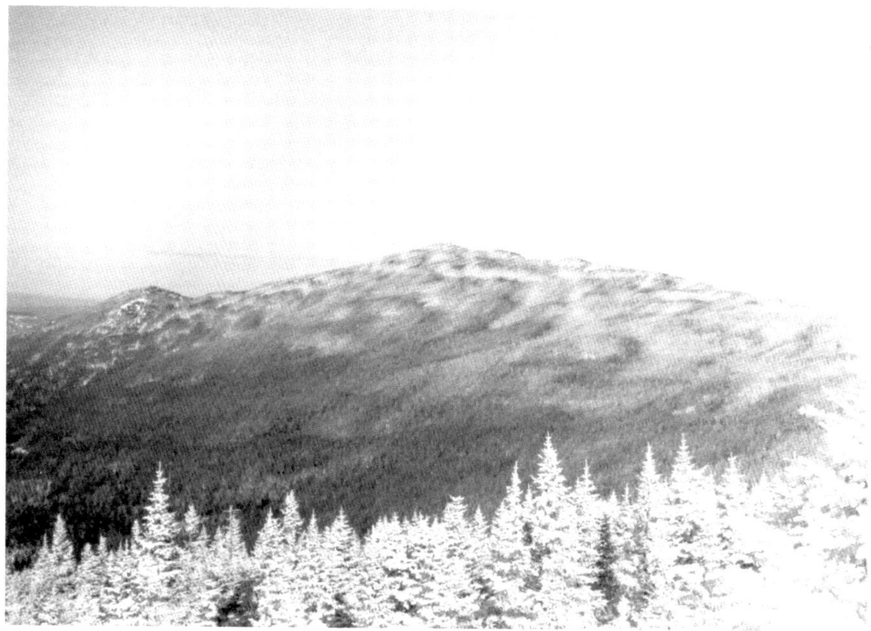

Fir waves on Esther Mountain.

When the dead trees finally fall to the ground, they start to rot. The rotting wood provides nutrients for seedlings. And that hole in the forest lets more sunlight hit the forest floor. This helps the new trees grow faster.

Year by year, the young trees grow taller and thicker. They begin to form a green covering over the opening in the forest. This fresh, green stripe follows the gray stripe up the mountainside.

That is a fir wave.

"It is all part of what is natural," said Dr. Ketchledge. It has probably been going on in high-elevation forests since the last ice age.

We have just been too busy watching waves at the ocean!

Gifford Pinchot: Walrus of the Forest

When New York State governor Theodore Roosevelt needed advice about management of the state's forests in 1899, who did he call? The man who created the science of forestry management in America, the chief of the Forestry Division in the U.S. Department of Agriculture: Gifford Pinchot.

And what did the two men do? They talked forestry, and they wrestled. Roosevelt won. Then they boxed, and Pinchot "had the honor of knocking the future president of the United States off his very solid pins."

Like Roosevelt, Pinchot was an avid sportsman and conservationist and hailed from a wealthy family. His father was a successful New York dry goods merchant and his mother an heiress. The young Pinchot could have lollygagged and drunk champagne all his days. He could have studied law or some other gentlemanly profession. Instead, after graduating from Yale, he chose to combine science with his love of hiking, camping and fishing in the woods. He chose to study forestry.

In the 1870s and 1880s, forest management and conservation were unheard of in the United States. American forests were thought to be inexhaustible. Wooded hillsides were clear-cut, debris heaped tens of feet high and nothing replanted. "Cut and run" was the standard practice.

Pinchot wanted to change that, but the United States had no schools of forestry. His father decided to send him to Europe. He studied with Sir

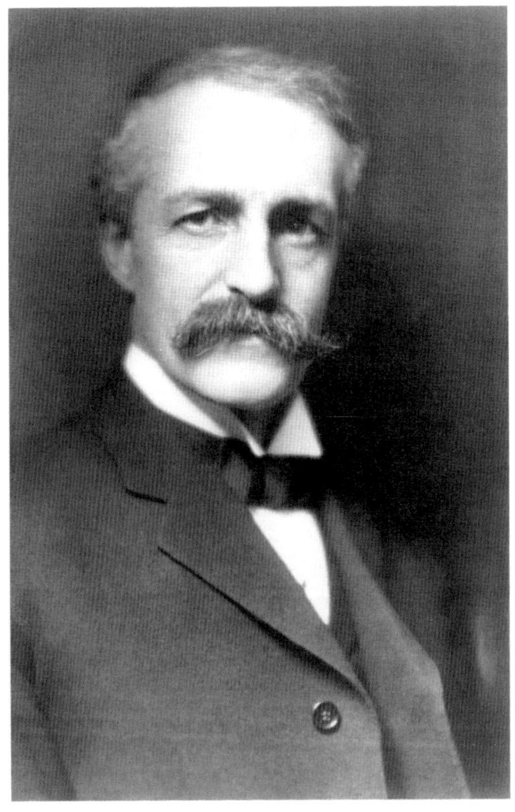

Gifford Pinchot. *U.S. Forest Service.*

Dietrich Brandis, the German authority on silviculture, attended the French Forest School and apprenticed with the best foresters in Europe. Upon his return to the family chateau in northeastern Pennsylvania in 1891, Pinchot set out to prove that American landowners' ruinous forestry practices were unnecessary; forest lands could both produce timber for harvest and remain forest for future generations.

As manager of George W. Vanderbilt's private five thousand acres of timberland in North Carolina, Pinchot began to earn a reputation as a forester—the first professionally trained scientific American forester. He strove to define that role, for the American public knew little about it. He recalled one lady saying to him, "So you are a forester! How very nice! Then you can tell me just what to do about my roses."

Those people who did know something about forestry, the various Forestry Associations, were working toward a different doctrine. They called it forestry, but Pinchot called it preservation. "They hated to see a tree cut down," wrote Pinchot. "So do I, and the chances are that you do too. But you cannot practice Forestry without it."

Pinchot believed forests and rivers should be used to fill practical needs, like supplying timber and power. He defined conservation as the wise use of the earth and its resources for the lasting good of men. He reasoned that "the greatest good for the greatest number in the long run" could be derived by scientifically managing the cutting of forests since this would provide profits and jobs today and protect resources for generations to come.

In 1892, Pinchot demonstrated this practice on William Seward Webb's forty-thousand-acre Ne-Ha-Sa-Ne Park in the western Adirondacks. Pinchot's survey of the land revealed a large stand of valuable spruce where older trees overshadowed younger ones. By carefully planned cutting, the production of wood actually increased year after year.

Pinchot made more studies of Ne-Ha-Sa-Ne Park and published *The Adirondack Spruce*, the first working plan for Adirondack landowners and lumbermen. Its tables of growth, volume and yield enabled foresters to predict the composition of forests in ten, twenty and thirty years based on present cutting practices.

Besides possessing expert forestry skills, Pinchot had great leadership characteristics. He was tall, thin, good looking and had zealous determination. Fellow workers in the Department of Agriculture's Forestry Division said, "He could outride and outshoot any ranger on the force."

In the Adirondacks, Pinchot demonstrated that he could out climb anyone, too. After meeting with Roosevelt in Albany in February 1899, Pinchot

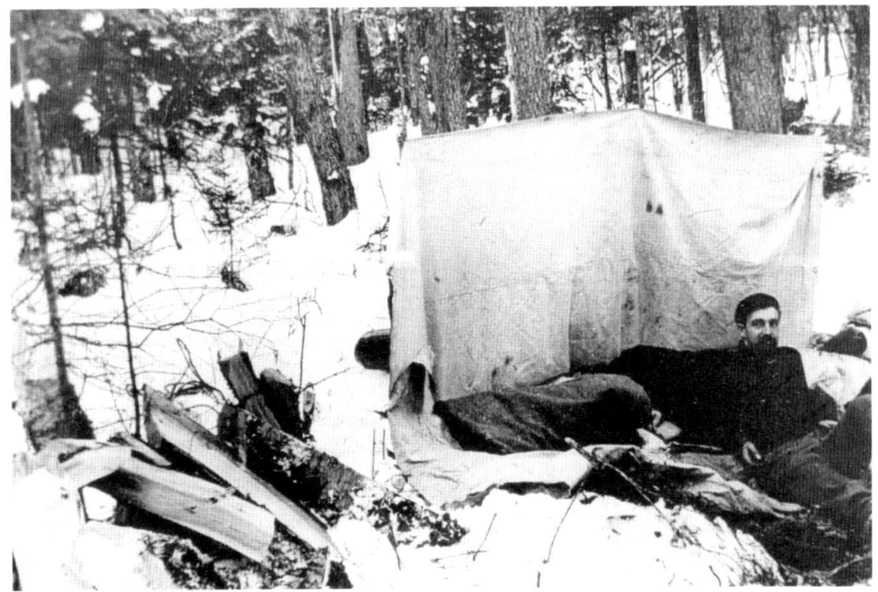

Gifford Pinchot in snow camp, 1898. *U.S. Forest Service.*

headed north to look over some forests for the Adirondack League Club. He and his companion, C. Grant LaFarge, a wealthy Boston architect, had a "delightful drive to Tahawus," though they overturned on the way. The men spent a week camped on a remote lake just southwest of Mount Marcy, the highest mountain in the state. The idea of climbing Mount Marcy in the deep snow was tossed around as a sort of joke, although it was thought that "it might be pleasanter to let it wait, say until June." After a time, though, the idea gained a firm hold on the two men. Despite cold temperatures, raging winds and the fact that a winter ascent had only been accomplished once before, they set off with two guides to climb Mount Marcy.

As they snowshoed through the dense woods, LaFarge wrote:

> [W]*e could enjoy now the exhilarating purity of the air, the frosty aroma of the balsam. The immaculate beauty of the snow itself and its many wonderful forms; the hushed silence; the many records of the feet of passing animals and birds; the sweet notes of the friendly chick-a-dees; the varied colors and textures of tree trunks and sumptuous richness of the evergreens, and the air that is like new life; all these rejoice the eye and the heart.*

The party of four reached Lake Tear of the Clouds at noon and ate lunch, standing on twenty feet of snow. LaFarge indicated that he thought it would be no great task to go to the top, so off they went. Before long, the guides gave up and returned to Lake Tear; one claimed his leg had gone numb, and the other said his snowshoes were too long.

Pinchot and LaFarge pushed on alone. At timberline, "the wind was no more to be faced than a battery of charging razors," wrote LaFarge, "and to stand upright in it was more than we cared to attempt." They left their snowshoes and crawled up the glare ice on all fours, making hand and foot holds by breaking through the ice.

"Foolish," Pinchot wrote in his diary. The cold was between twenty-five and forty degrees below zero, he estimated. It became unbearable for LaFarge. Just two hundred feet below the summit, he turned around and crawled down the slope. He stomped in the snow to try to return circulation to his frozen feet.

Meanwhile, Pinchot crawled to the signal pole marking the highest point of New York State. Acres and acres of forest were beneath the chief of the U.S. Forestry Division, but the view was hidden in fog; he saw nothing but snow and ice.

When the men returned to the safety of the forest, they looked at each other and laughed at their peculiar appearance. Icicles hung on their eyelashes, and with Pinchot's beard solidly coated with ice, he looked like a walrus. He later discovered that he had made the ascent during the famous blizzard of 1899.

In September 1901, Theodore Roosevelt became president of the United States just hours after he descended the same slopes of Mount Marcy, when President McKinley died from a pistol wound. As president, Roosevelt reorganized the management of the national forests, creating the United States Forest Service and appointing Pinchot to the powerful job of chief forester.

During his reign, Pinchot implemented his conservation policy and increased the national forests from 60 to 193 million acres. Not everyone agreed with Pinchot's objectives or methods at the Forest Service. Conservationist John Muir wanted the national forests to be off limits to lumbering, livestock grazing and dam construction. He wanted them preserved for their beauty. Muir wanted to stop the axe; Pinchot wanted to regulate its use.

Pinchot won the battle on the national level but not in New York State. Article VII, now Article XIV, of the state constitution, known as the "Forever Wild" clause, forbids the cutting of any tree in the Adirondack State Forest Preserve.

President William Howard Taft, Roosevelt's successor in the White House, fired Pinchot for insubordination in 1910. Pinchot returned home to Milford, Pennsylvania, and entered state politics. He served two terms as governor of Pennsylvania, in 1923 and 1931.

Though he enjoyed being head of the state, it was not his first love. At age seventy, Pinchot said, "I have…been a Governor, every now and then, but I am a forester all the time—have been, shall be, all my working life."

Pinchot was a forester all the time—whether fighting to stop sloppy timber practices, surveying Adirondack spruce or snowshoeing through an icy blizzard on Mount Marcy.

Wilderness Reflections

Going Wild Over Thoreau

Every summer, just before the Fourth of July, I feel Thoreau nudging me to go "live deep and suck out all the marrow of life." I pack up my family—two giggly girls, two cats, two goldfish, one husband—and, with a canoe on the roof and a plywood trailer hitched behind, our truck inches toward our camp in the Adirondack woods.

In my humble log hut, I can practice my writing craft and "front only the essential facts of life" as Thoreau did. The first night, I confront the essentialness of heat. The depiction of log cabins as warm and cozy ignores the reality of settling cracks, insect infestation and water seepage. Thoreau asked, "Cold and damp—are they not as rich experience as warmth and dryness?" And so I soak up the richness in wool underwear, down comforter and fleece ski mask.

This isn't exactly what my friends back in suburbia envision. When I tell them that I spend summers writing in my cabin in the Adirondack Mountains, their eyes get cloudy. Lips curl into smiles. I watch as Henry David Thoreau dances across their visage, plunges into Walden Pond and then transforms into me. They envision me sitting at an old oak desk, staring out the open window pondering the mysteries of life and the subtleties of nature. Sparrows flutter about the pine branches. Deer lap water at the pond's edge. The soft swish of aspens, the peeper's trill and the music of lead on paper resound through my writer's heaven.

Of course, those same visions lured me to the writing profession. As Thoreau preached, "If one advances confidently in the direction of his

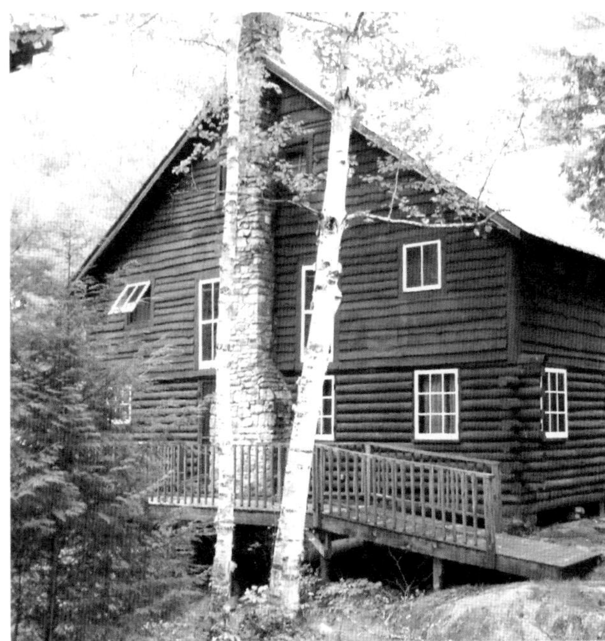

Sandra Weber's cabin in the woods.

dreams, and endeavors to live the life which he has imagined, he will meet with a success unexpected in common hours." So I bought a cabin in the woods and endeavored to make my living as a writer.

While Thoreau shunned society's pretty toys, I cannot shun technology. I need my computer and printer. And dare I mention my hair dryer, alarm clock and coffee machine? Part of the mystique of my life is accurate. My desk is oak—an oak-laminate computer table. Like Thoreau, I drink spring water and eat sweet corn and wild berries. Five raspberries, to be exact. That's how many I picked on my last foraging expedition before the girls screamed, "Prickers!"

A search for silence is hopeless; I'd settle for an hour of quiet. My cabin is one hundred yards from Route 9, a major roadway by Adirondack standards. The pines and birches soften the sound, but eighteen-wheelers make the aspens quake and the log walls shake. At night, when the road noise subsides, the music of mosquitoes hovers above my tender ears. Their hum resonates like a buzz saw.

Thoreau loved to spend time observing wild animals. He called them his brute neighbors; they are my wild housemates. From my bed, I study carpenter ants as they reengineer a corner joint. What diligent workers—undeterred by stone pillars, insecticide and ultrasonic pulses. "We need the tonic of wildness," wrote Thoreau. "We must be refreshed by the sight of inexhaustible vigor." The ants refresh me—or is it cool air wafting through the hole in the log? Although I never communed with Thoreau's woodchuck or fox, their friends are here. Mice peek from the closet. Flying squirrels flutter about the loft. Other wildlife leave gifts: turkey droppings under the clothesline, bird splatterings on my lawn chair and deer dung in the driveway.

Thoreau also had little fishy friends that swam in Walden's sweet water. Loons bathed there, too, making the early morning woods ring with wild laughter. I have no calm, clear pond. However, after rainstorms, I have a river in the driveway. And every morning my woods ring with wild screeches of little girls battling over bed blankets.

Some days, I stare out the window pondering the mysteries of no-see-ums and the subtleties of composting toilets. Other days, I spend pleasant hours listening to the rain on the tin roof accompanied by twenty-seven verses to "Itsy-Bitsy Spider." At day's end, I echo Thoreau: "And lo, it is evening, and nothing memorable is accomplished."

As for solitude, Thoreau thrived on it; I am deprived of it. At my cabin, I am never alone, only lonesome. My husband returns to suburbia most weeks, and I am left to single-handedly entertain my daughters, solve home maintenance problems and cater to visiting relatives. "To be in company, even with the best, is soon wearisome and dissipating."

Between the six-course dinners for ten, the overtaxed septic tank, loads of bed laundry, catfights and broken water pipes, I manage to scribble a few lines. My best writing is accomplished in the morning, for "morning is when I am awake and there is a dawn in me." At 5:00 a.m. I throw off sleep, pry open my eyelids and plop in front of the computer. I enjoy three or four hours of productive writing before the traffic starts. If the girls don't squeal for breakfast. If the cats don't wrestle the squirrels. If the mice don't chew the power cord.

Oh, I savor the Thoreau mystique at my log cabin. Each summer is an opportunity for reflection and creative thinking. Then, on Labor Day, some magnetism in nature directs me to head south. I leave the woods for as good a reason as I went there. I have lived deep and sucked out all the marrow of the mystique.

Achievement

This past year [1992], I climbed my first Adirondack peaks. As I reached the top of each mountain, I was filled with great awe at my personal accomplishment. I had climbed rocks and ridges. I had endured the pain in my knees and blisters on my feet.

I basked in the morning sun a mile above sea level. I felt the north wind in my face. I tingled from my balaclava to my Rockports. I reveled in my achievement.

Later, while working on a research paper about motivation, I saw a picture of Vigeland's *The Fountain*. This sculpture, in Oslo, Norway, is said to demonstrate that achievement is not an individual thing, even though it may appear that the work and energy is of only one person, but that achievement is the cumulative effort of many bodies and brains—even of all mankind.

Suddenly, I looked at my achievements in a new way. I reflected on who and what make them happen—the cumulative effort of many bodies and brains that put me on top of Phelps, Marcy, Giant, Algonquin, Cascade, Porter and the rest.

My first thoughts were of Uncle Gerhard. His recent death had inspired me to return to the Adirondacks about which he talked so much. I thought of my parents, who reared me and gave me a love for the woods. My husband had provided companionship and compassion during the hikes.

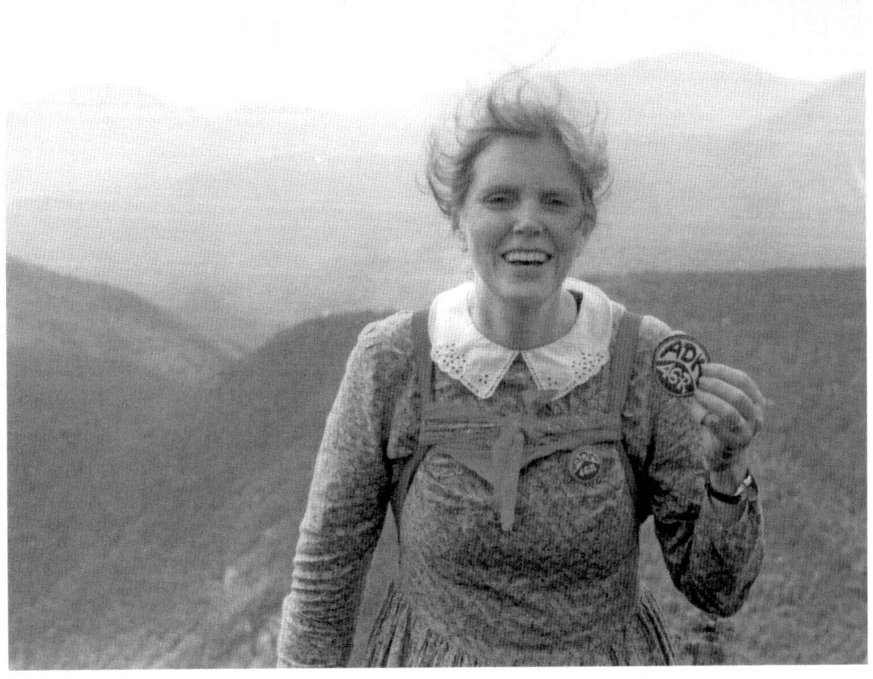

Sandra Weber achieving her forty-sixth peak, Nippletop Mountain, in 2003.

Then, I thought of all the nameless people who had a part in creating this trail system. The hikers before me were respectful and thoughtful; they left the woods undisturbed and unmarked by their passing. Many diligent, caring people worked on the trails to maintain safe access to the peaks. Callused hands and aching backs forged a path for all to enjoy the splendor of the woods.

Generations of selfless, conservation-minded people fought with their words, hands and money to protect and preserve the Adirondacks. Hence, it was possible for me to ascend these glorious mountains this year.

I am certain that when I reach my next peak, I will reflect on the cumulative effort of the many bodies and brains that contributed to "our" achievement. See you at the top—and thanks.

Dividing Lines

Looking down Route 10A, I'm not really sure why I insisted that we add another hour to our trip so I could stop here. I feel better as I leave the car and walk toward Caroga Creek, with my husband and daughter following behind.

My ears hear Emily asking, "Daddy, where are we going?" My eyes are peeled for a glimpse of our destination—a place frequently discussed, cursed and heralded but seldom seen. Finally, I find it—the Blue Line. The "Entering Adirondack Park" sign clearly states that this is the park boundary.

I walk past Caroga Creek and stand next to the sign, one foot on each side of the Blue Line, letting the sensation tingle up my legs and into my heart. It fills my ears with gurgles and tweets and rustles; my eyes with butterflies and birch, goldenrod and golden sun; my nose with clover and pine.

Time passes by. A bobwhite passes by. Butterflies pass by. Ripples pass by. Pickup trucks pass by.

I feel like a tiny speck in this grand mass of space, history and science.

I had this feeling once before, standing on the Continental Divide in the Canadian Rockies. From Lake Louise, we drove to the little town of Stephen and then out a narrow road. From there, we walked down a paved path to a tiny stream, stopping at the spot marked by a cairn and a big sign:

Canadian Pacific Railway
The Great Divide
Altitude 5332 ft.
Alberta / British Columbia Boundary

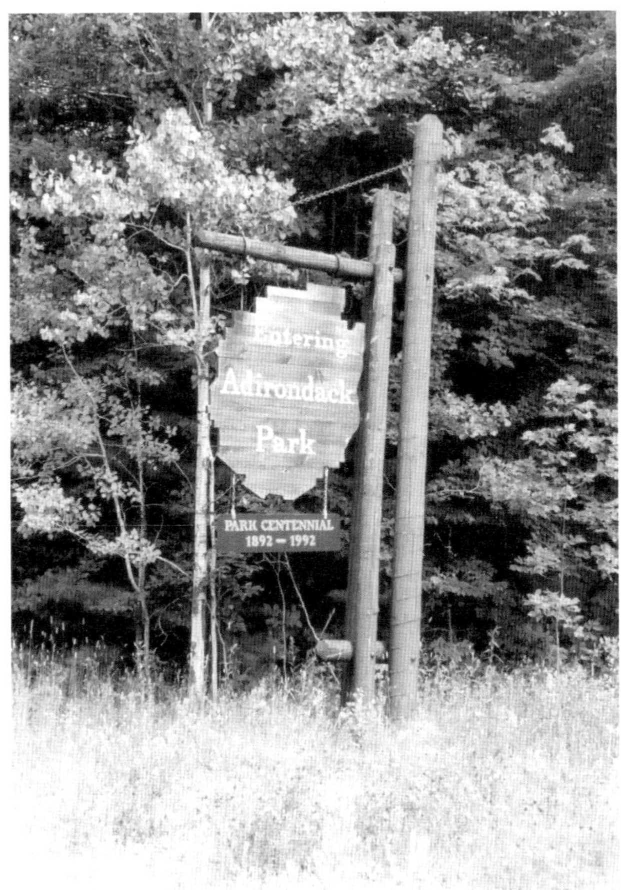

An Adirondack Park sign marking the boundary of the Blue Line. (NOTE: there are signs at various border points.)

A smaller sign explained the "Parting of the Waters" attraction—the unusual, unnamed stream divided naturally into two parts, one headed to the Pacific Ocean and the other to the Atlantic. The Great Divide also separated British Columbia to the west from Alberta to the east.

It wasn't very impressive. It was just a little trickle of water, nothing significant like Hoover Dam or Niagara Falls, Old Faithful or the Grand Canyon.

The simplicity amazed me. As I stood there beside the Canadian rails that would return me to Vancouver, the natural order of the world seemed as clear as that small stream. All the secrets of the earth seemed concentrated at that spot and pouring out in that little trickle of water.

Each trickle of meltwater went by, suspended for an instant—its destiny hanging in the air—and then dropped. It was on its way to Lake Wapta, down Kicking Horse River, to the Columbia River and out to the Pacific

Ocean. Or its journey may be across Canada via the Bow River, to the South Saskatchewan River, into Hudson Bay and out to the Atlantic Ocean.

In nature, things just happen; in a split second, destinies are decided. That's the way it has always been. The trickle follows its course, whether north or west. It doesn't complain or grieve. It accepts its destiny and rejoices in its purposefulness in the world.

Now, as I stand on the Blue Line, the secrets of the park unfold. They come from that concentrated bank on Caroga Creek. When I cross the line to the north, I am headed for silence, slowness, freedom, history, feldspar, virgin spruce, wilderness, alpine tundra.

To the south of the line, I head for civilization. There are cities and factories and clocks and trucks and universities and hospitals and operas and art museums.

The Blue Line is a great divide in my life; part of my life trickles to wilderness and part trickles to civilization. Each tributary fills a purpose in my soul and the world.

Like the water drops that cross the Great Divide and voyage to the ocean to be evaporated, condensed and precipitated onto the Great Divide again, I am reborn to a new destiny each time I cross the Blue Line. I am thankful I took the time to stop and enjoy the sensation of that split second.

Clear Pond

No visit to the Adirondack Mountains seems complete without a walk on the dock at Heart Lake. I drive five long miles, down the deserted road, through rows of red pines and dark green balsams. At last, I sit on the quiet bench at the end of the dock and peer at the scenery. Tall white birches reach toward the cloudless blue sky. Farther in the distance, the hearty firs cover the mountainsides with their luxuriant blankets.

Loud *wonk-wonks* interrupt the peace. My eyes search for the source of the quarrel and spot three ravens riding the air currents. They soar toward the rocky cliffs of Mount Jo. It is not an exceptionally tall mountain—less than three thousand feet high—but its flat, open top provides an exceptional view of the surrounding high peaks.

I look up at Jo's summit, and it looks out to Avalanche and Algonquin Peak, Rocky Falls and Indian Pass, Mount Marcy and Wallface. From the wooden bench on Heart Lake, I feel the essence of the Adirondack wilderness sinking into my bones.

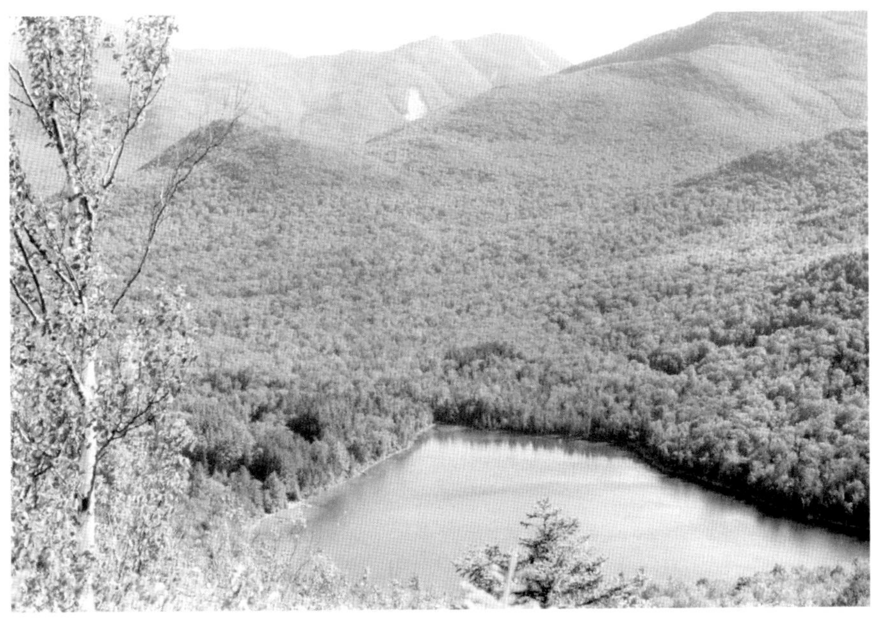

Heart Lake from Mount Jo.

Fulfilled, and obedient of "Old Mountain" Phelps tenet to not "hog down the view," I sit back and look at the water before me. I see why Heart Lake used to be called Clear Pond. The water is unruffled and serene, the surface like a looking glass. And reflected onto it are graceful birch forms, the craggy face of Mount Jo and sublime sky blueness.

The pond is so crystal clear that I find it perplexing. I realize that I cannot tell what is real and what is a reflection. Which is the forest and which is the lake?

After I ponder, I wonder—does it matter? Clearly, nature's reflection is as beautiful as the real form, perhaps even more beautiful.

It makes me wonder about *my* reflection. I think about the image reflected back by my words and actions. The way I treat the waters and woods, the way I treat strangers and friends. The words I write, the songs I sing, the lessons I teach my children. The roads I avoid and the trails I blaze.

I wonder what will be cast back if my form strikes the water's surface. How will Nature reflect me? Dare I look into the clear waters before me, or should I go look in Mud Pond?

Slowly, I gather courage, look down onto Clear Pond and probe for my portrayal.

Sources

Hooked on History

Originally published in the *Sequel* [Paul Smith's College] (Spring/Summer 2001).

Lake Tear

Originally published in *New York State Conservationist* (August 2009).

Passed By

First appeared in *Adirondack Life* 32, no. 6 (September/October 2001).

Roosevelt's Ride

Originally appeared in *Mount Marcy, The High Peak of New York*. Fleischmanns, NY: Purple Mountain Press, Ltd., 2001.

Up Herbert Brook

Originally appeared in *Two in the Wilderness*. Calkins Creek Books/Boyds Mills Press, Inc., 2005.

Call it Tahawus

Originally appeared in *Mount Marcy, The High Peak of New York*. Fleischmanns, NY: Purple Mountain Press, Ltd., 2001.

Who Was Jo?

Originally published in *Adirondac* (January/February 1999).

Mount Van Hoevenberg

Originally appeared in *The Finest Square Mile, Mount Jo and Heart Lake*. Fleischmanns, NY: Purple Mountain Press, Ltd., 1998.

Fare-Thee-Well

Originally appeared in *Mount Marcy, The High Peak of New York*. Fleischmanns, NY: Purple Mountain Press, Ltd., 2001.

Writing Gone Astray

Originally published in *SCBWI Bulletin* (May/June 1999).

Girl Gone Wild

First appeared in *Adirondack Life* 36, no. 3 (May/June 2005).

MARTHA REBEN, WILDERNESS HEALTH SEEKER

Originally appeared in *Breaking Trail, Remarkable Women of the Adirondacks* (co-author, Peggy Lynn). Fleischmanns, NY: Purple Mountain Press, Ltd., 2004.

THE LADIES AND THE TRAMP

First appeared in *Adirondack Life* 33, no. 4 (Annual Guide 2002).

GRACE HUDOWALSKI, FORTY-SIXER #9

Originally appeared in *Breaking Trail, Remarkable Women of the Adirondacks* (co-author, Peggy Lynn). Fleischmanns, NY: Purple Mountain Press, Ltd., 2004.

THE BIG BURN

First appeared in *Adirondack Life* 34, no. 2 (March/April 2003).

AT DUCK HOLE

Originally appeared in *Two in the Wilderness*. Calkins Creek Books/Boyds Mills Press, Inc., 2005.

SAVIOR OF THE SUMMITS

Initially appeared in *Adirondack Explorer* (July 1999).

FIR WAVES

Originally published in *WOW (Wild Outdoor World)* (September/October 2001).

Gifford Pinchot

Originally published in *New York State Conservationist* (December 2000).

Going Wild Over Thoreau

Initially appeared in *Adirondack Explorer* (July 2000).

Achievement

Originally published in *Adirondac* (Winter 1992–93).

Dividing Lines

Originally published in *Adirondac* (July/August 1994).

About the Author

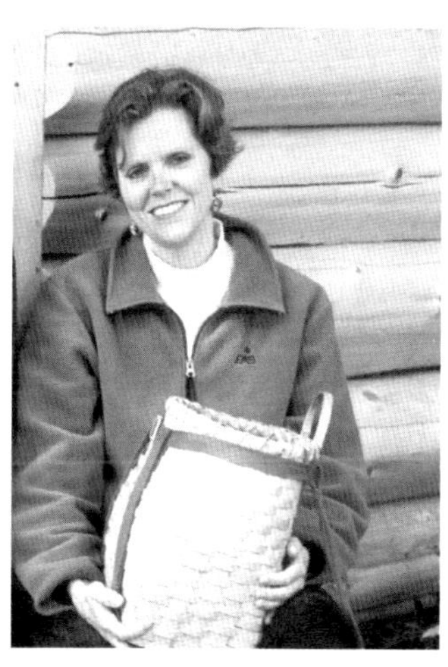

Sandra Weber has been a part-time Adirondacks resident for fifteen years (her other residence is in Lansdale, Pennsylvania). Since her first visit, she fell in love with the region and has published many books and articles on it. In addition, Sandra is a member of the following organizations and has presented book-related programs for them: Adirondack Museum, Adirondack Mountain Club, Adirondack Forty-Sixers and Adirondack History Center. She is also well known for her "Mountain Women" performances with folksinger Peggy Lynn. They have presented at venues throughout upstate New York, including the Adirondack Museum, the Schroon Lake Folk Festival, the Field and Stream Festival, the Chronicle Book Fair in Glens Falls, SUNY Oswego, Paul Smith's College, Bluseed Studios, Tannery Pond Community Center and various schools and libraries.

Her books have been reviewed in *Adirondac*, *New York State Conservationist*, *Albany Times Union*, *Adirondack Explorer*, *Adirondack Life* and various local papers. She has been interviewed on North Country NPR radio and on Albany's *Women's Voices* program.